HELPLESS VICTIM

Farah Fratta woke in the early hours of the morning to find a man in a black ski mask standing over her. She let out a piercing shriek and sat up, waking her young son who was sleeping next to her.

"I've come to talk about Bob," the intruder said. He was holding a small black object and carrying a bottle of Tequila.

Her scream had wakened her two other small children and they ran into the center of the room crying.

"Whatever you are going to do, please don't do it in front of my children," the terrified mother sobbed.

The man pushed the children out of the bedroom and closed the door. He ordered Farah to turn over, then jerked down her nightgown and jabbed a black stun gun against her bare skin. She screamed in intense pain.

The stun gun jabbed her throat, searing it with an electrical charge. Farah screamed again as the smell of scorched skin filled the room.

BOOK YOUR PLACE ON OUR WEBSITE AND MAKE THE READING CONNECTION!

We've created a customized website just for our very special readers, where you can get the inside scoop on everything that's going on with Zebra, Pinnacle and Kensington books.

When you come online, you'll have the exciting opportunity to:

- View covers of upcoming books
- Read sample chapters
- Learn about our future publishing schedule (listed by publication month *and author*)
- Find out when your favorite authors will be visiting a city near you
- Search for and order backlist books from our online catalog
- Check out author bios and background information
- Send e-mail to your favorite authors
- Meet the Kensington staff online
- Join us in weekly chats with authors, readers and other guests
- Get writing guidelines
- AND MUCH MORE!

**Visit our website at
http://www.pinnaclebooks.com**

NO SAFE PLACE

BILL G. COX

Pinnacle Books
Kensington Publishing Corp.
http://www.pinnaclebooks.com

Some names have been changed to protect the privacy of individuals connected to this story.

PINNACLE BOOKS are published by

Kensington Publishing Corp.
850 Third Avenue
New York, NY 10022

Pinnacle and the P logo Reg. U.S. Pat. & TM Off.

First Printing: January, 2000
10

Printed in the United States of America

This book is dedicated to, as always,
my wife, Nina.

ONE

The people chatting together in the living room of the comfortable, two-story home had no inkling of the terror that was about to erupt.

A young married couple, Daren and Laura Hoelscher and their nine-month-old son, Caleb, and Laura's friend, Elizabeth Campbell and her twelve-year-old daughter Crystal, had just returned in separate cars from attending Wednesday night church services and other activities.

It was a typically quiet, late autumn evening for the two families, who, to economize, shared the home and the expenses. Their house on Timbers Trail was in the residential subdivision of Atascocita, a developing area near oil-famous Humble, Texas.

Laura Hoelscher had been the last to come in, having dropped by her beauty salon to get a permanent.

"Hi, everybody. I'm here," she said, stooping to pick up her baby. He woke up and started to cry.

"He went to sleep in his car seat," her husband said. "So I just left him in it."

"Now, now, here I am, honey," the mother cooed, cuddling the tearful infant in her arms. "It's dinner time, isn't it, baby." She dropped to a couch beside her husband to breast-feed the baby and tell Daren about her day.

The couch was in the middle of the room, facing two large picture windows. The windows offered a panoramic view of the neighborhood, and mini-blinds on the windows were always kept raised.

Elizabeth Campbell and her daughter were sitting on another nearby couch. As they talked casually, Campbell saw a car turn the corner, its headlights sweeping momentarily into the room. The car slowed, stopped and then backed into the driveway of the two-story house across the street.

The remote-control door on the attached garage whirred upward and Campbell saw the automatic light inside come on and the driver guide the car inside. She recognized the driver as a neighbor, Farah Fratta, a pretty young woman who worked for American Airlines in downtown Houston, the big metropolis thirty miles to the south and slightly west.

Theirs was only a casual relationship, a "wave hello and good-bye" sort of thing. Elizabeth and the Hoelschers knew that Farah had three small children and was separated from their father.

On weekends and occasionally during the week, they would see the father pick up or bring home the three Fratta youngsters, two boys and a girl; the parents shared custody apparently, not an unusual domestic situation these days. Farah Fratta's husband—was his name Bob?—looked to be a pleasant enough man, but they knew him by sight only. They understood he was some kind of police officer in nearby Missouri City, Texas.

Having observed the neighbor come home, Campbell turned again to the conversation in the room. Suddenly there was a sharp, loud *pop* from the direction of the house across the street. Then a scream, followed immediately by another loud report.

Daren Hoelscher got up and went to the front door to look out. "Must be kids shooting off firecrackers and cutting up," he said.

Laura Hoelscher, nursing her now contented and gurgling baby, had also seen Farah Fratta drive into her garage.

She jumped at the sound of the first loud *pop,* followed by the scream and the second explosive sound. She was startled to see Farah Fratta fall to the garage floor beside her car. Then came the shocking realization—Laura had seen a shooting!

With her gaze riveted on the tableau in the garage some fifty feet across the street, she thought for an instant that she glimpsed part of some red clothing that might be someone at the back of the car. But it was such a fleeting impression she was not certain. It was the woman lying on the floor who held her spellbound.

"She's shot! She's shot!" Laura cried.

The baby in her arms started wailing as the stunned mother exclaimed again: "Farah's shot!"

Hearing the urgency in his wife's voice, Daren Hoelscher hurried to the windows for a better view of the house across the street. "Maybe Farah and her kids are playing a game," he said, thinking that might explain what they had heard—firecrackers and the mother feigning a fall to the floor. But that seemed pretty far out. And he didn't see any kids. He noticed that the car in the garage was not the car that the neighbor usually drove. It was a 1994 white Nissan Maxima. He knew Farah Fratta drove a 1991 Honda Accord.

Getting to her feet, Campbell asked incredulously,

"Shot! Are you sure, Laura?" She moved to the window for a better view.

"Yes! Yes! I'm sure! I saw her fall! Can you see her? See, there on the floor by the car!" Hoelscher stood up, starting to cry and patting her crying baby. "She needs to get up! If she doesn't get up, I'm calling 911! I'm calling!" She blurted these words, at the same time rushing into the kitchen to get the phone. It had a long cord and she dialed the emergency number as she returned to the windows.

The operator came on the line immediately. Hoelscher interrupted her own phone call, her voice rising up the scale: "Look! There's somebody standing by that tree!"

She could see a shadowy figure to the left of a tree and large bush at the side of Farah's house, near the corner of the back fence and several feet left of the lighted garage.

"Do you see him? He's outside, left of that tree at the side. He's crouched down and moving back of the tree now! See him?"

As they watched, the witnesses saw a small flare of red light, lasting only seconds, near the large bush where Laura Hoelscher said she saw a man. She sounded near hysteria as she told the 911 operator: "A woman's been shot and I see a man in her yard!!"

The figure in the dark suddenly stood up. "There he is, can you see him? Can you see him?" Laura cried.

"No, I can't see him. Where is he?" asked Campbell.

"Right there in front, standing in front of the bush!"

Elizabeth Campbell stared for a few seconds before she spotted something in the area.

"Yes, I can see him, I see him now!" she said, although all she could make out was the dark figure of a medium-built person. There wasn't enough light for her to distinguish any facial features or clothing color. But she did see his hand make a fidgety movement.

Oh, Lord, does he have a gun in his hand? she wondered.

The blurred form moved toward the street and was illuminated by a tall vapor light on the corner.

Daren Hoelscher saw him, too, a weird-looking night apparition that seemed to be prancing or hopping from the bush toward the street curb. A lithe, twisting figure in a black shirt, black pants, with something black covering his head and face, or he was a black man.

The man looked to be medium size. Laura Hoelscher thought he had a "very round" head, as she would later describe the phantom prowler to the police.

The figure twisted and twitched. His hands were clasped together in front, working nervously as he did that strange hoppety gait toward the street that separated them.

"He's coming this way!" Laura Hoelscher exclaimed.

The man in black reached the street curb, paused and looked to his right toward the corner, then faded back into the darkness.

Daren Hoelscher started to open the door and look out, but was halted by his wife's sharp warning, "Don't go out there, Daren! I don't see him anywhere. He may be in our yard now."

The light in Farah's garage went out, probably automatically as such lights do—or had someone turned it out, they wondered? Their own vulnerable position dawned on the transfixed witnesses. All of the lights in their house were on, and they were standing there looking out the windows with the blinds wide open, watching for somebody who seemingly had just shot down a woman!

Had the gunman or an accomplice turned off the light, realizing belatedly that the bizarre shooting had been played out on a fully lighted stage?

The gunman easily could have spotted them and be headed their way at this moment. They were sitting ducks in the brightness of their home's illumination with all the shades up.

"Turn the lights off! Douse the lights!" Daren Hoelscher yelled through the commotion in the living room. With his wife crying and brokenly talking to the 911 operator at the same time, he and Elizabeth Campbell ran through the rooms switching off lights and locking doors. He locked the door to their own garage.

Campbell took the sobbing baby from the arms of his mother, who continued to describe the events to the 911 dispatcher. She grasped her own weeping daughter's hand and took the children upstairs. She put them in a bathroom that had no window on the other side of the house. She hoped it was the safest place in the house.

Meanwhile, as the Hoelschers watched from the now darkened living room, a car whipped around the corner on Timbers Trail and stopped at the Fratta driveway. The man in black ran from the bush and jumped into the passenger seat of the small, silver car that had pulled up. Daren Hoelscher noticed that the car had only one working headlight. He couldn't see the driver clearly.

As the vehicle took off, he ran outside to try to

get the license number, but trees along the street prevented him from getting a full view of the accelerating car. He could only tell it was a white license, a Texas plate, but he could not make out the numerals.

When Campbell came back downstairs, Daren Hoelscher was standing at the bottom step, near the front door. Campbell said she had heard a car drive away fast. To her, it sounded as if it traveled around from Timber Trails to Spoonwood, a nearby street.

Hoelscher said, "They're gone. What do we do now? Laura and I saw the car stop at Farah's driveway. The man ran out and jumped in. I couldn't tell much about the driver. They left pretty fast, and that's probably all of them. I think we should go over there and see if we can help Farah."

He also wanted to check on Farah's children, because they had not been seen.

Had their mother interrupted a burglary and suffered the consequences? What was the fate of her two small sons and little daughter? Had they been at home with a baby-sitter in the house? Were they injured, or worse?

There were too many unknowns, too much at stake for the mother and possibly the youngsters. Campbell agreed they should do something to try to help the hapless shooting victim, whose blood was ebbing away on the garage floor, and find out about her children.

It was dark in their own garage, and they could not find a flashlight. Hoelscher grabbed a can of Mace by the front door, and he and Campbell hurried outside. Laura remained behind to look after the children.

They still could not decide how they were going

to approach the Frattas' open but now darkened garage with as much caution as possible. They wished they had a weapon other than the Mace.

Hoelscher said, "I'm going to back my car out, turn it around and shine the lights into her garage, and we can see if anyone else is still in there."

"Don't you think I ought to go get some more help?" Campbell asked.

"Yeah, maybe you should," said Hoelscher as he switched on his car's ignition. He backed out and turned around to direct his headlights into the Fratta garage. Campbell ran down the block to the home of a family who, she recalled, had once remarked they knew and socialized with Farah Fratta's parents. They could notify the parents, she thought.

She glimpsed a small blue car with a bubble on top turn onto Timber Trails.

Assuming it probably was a paramedic, since Laura had already been on the phone for a few minutes with the 911 dispatcher, Campbell hailed the driver, shouting, "The woman who was shot is in that garage." She pointed to where Hoelscher now had parked his car in the Fratta driveway.

With his car's headlights spotlighting Farah's car and her body, Hoelscher knelt down beside her. She lay on her left side, her legs partly drawn up as if sleeping. Her body was parallel to the driver's side of the car. He saw that her head almost touched the left rear tire. A large puddle of blood was spreading around her head.

"Farah," Hoelscher said gently. No response at all. He touched her lightly on the hip. No reaction.

"Farah . . . Farah. Can you hear me?"

Her eyes were wide open, stationary, staring unseeing and unblinking, but he knew she was alive.

She was taking deep, gasping breaths that swelled her chest in and out like a manually operated bellows. Her skin was cool to the touch and looked pale in spite of her good tan. He noticed she was wearing her gym workout clothes: gray cotton shorts, a shirt and tennis shoes.

He was sure that she was a dying woman, and he did the only thing he could think of to do.

Instinctively, from his own Catholic faith, Hoelscher placed his finger lightly on her forehead and made the sign of the cross, quietly blessing her and administering last rites.

From where the blood was, Hoelscher believed she had been shot in the head. Then he ran outside to the curb and yelled to his wife that Farah was shot and dying.

He returned to his mission of trying to find the Fratta children. The first paramedic and a second who joined him had started working on the victim. One medic made a quick examination, then ran back to his unit to summon additional help and equipment, including the Life Flight helicopter.

When the medic came back, Hoelscher asked, "Do you think it's okay if I go check the house? I don't know whether her kids or other people might be in there."

The EMS man nodded.

Hoelscher left the garage by the side door, crossed a breezeway to the back door of the house. He found the door locked. He did not go around to test the front door because police officers had arrived and would do that. He saw nothing that looked like a forced entry.

By now police cars, more EMS vehicles, an ambulance, neighbors and other people were swarming in the neighborhood. Flashing blue-and-red emergency lights and the distant wailing of more sirens were making a nerve-jarring cacophony in the usually quiet residential area.

The medics worked frantically to save Farah Fratta's life. Only her legs were visible from the circle of EMS people and equipment.

Her legs were motionless.

TWO

Lex Baquer had been home from work about an hour, time enough to take a shower and sit down for dinner. His wife, Betty, turned on the TV to watch something on the Discovery Channel.

A few minutes past 8 P.M. on Wednesday, November 9, 1994, the telephone rang.

"Who the hell would be calling this time of evening?" Baquer asked. It had been a long day and he was a little grumpy. His wife answered the phone.

She heard the voice of Don Covington, a longtime friend and former neighbor when the Baquers first moved to Humble years ago. It sounded like he was crying.

"Don, what's wrong?" Betty Baquer asked, suddenly feeling alarmed.

"Farah has been shot!" Covington blurted. "Come quick."

She screamed.

Lex Baquer jumped to his feet. "What's wrong? What happened?"

"Farah has been shot!" his wife sobbed.

"Oh, my God!"

Later, Baquer would remember little of what took place next. He was in shock. With his crying wife beside him in their car, he switched on the emergency light and floored the gas pedal.

Fortunately, it was only three miles from their residence in Humble to where their daughter lived in Atascocita.

Police cars were everywhere, blocking off the street, parked at odd angles. Baquer saw an ambulance in the driveway of his daughter's house.

An officer with a flashlight stopped him. Baquer rolled down his window. "It's my daughter! She has been shot! Please, I must get through!"

The former Britisher was a distinguished-looking man, with his mustache and graying temples, and his words still carried a noticeable British clip, although he had been in America and lived in Texas for fifteen years. He gave the impression of a man people listened to when he spoke.

Before Baquer could start moving again, his wife opened her door and jumped from the car, kicked off her slippers and started running toward the lighted garage. She fell down three times during her desperate sprint and was helped up each time by people in the teeming crowd of spectators.

Reaching the yellow tape barrier, she was told she could go no farther.

"That's my daughter in there!" she cried and ducked under the tape.

An officer grabbed her. "Ma'am, you can't go in there."

"Don't you understand? It's my daughter, my daughter!" she cried. But she was still restrained from entering the garage where medics worked frantically over the prostrate form.

The distraught mother slumped to the street, her head in her hands, crying uncontrollably. A neighbor woman lifted her up and gently led her to a nearby home.

Somebody yelled to Lex Baquer, "Go that way!" Farther on, another uniformed officer tried to wave him down, but Baquer swung around him and pulled up almost in front of his daughter's house. He jumped out of the car and ran toward the garage. He could see medical workers beside Farah's car. The car was parked facing out.

He glimpsed his daughter, the lovely young woman he still affectionally called "Baby," on the floor next to her car. He started forward, but someone grabbed him from behind. "Please sir, you can't go in there."

"I must get to her!" he shouted. He wanted to get to her side, touch her, reassure her "Dad's here, Baby." He had never felt this helpless.

Again he caught a look at her. She was having convulsions, shaking so terribly. "Oh, my God, I must get to her," he moaned.

He was surrounded by Farah's neighbors, who knew him well and were trying to comfort him. The Baquers' son, Zain Baquer and his wife, Donna, had arrived in their car, but Lex Baquer was not sure where his wife or son were at this point.

All he could do was stare at the nightmarish scene, wanting what he was seeing not to be true. "Please, let me go to her," he said again.

Don Covington, the close friend who had called their house with the tragic message, put his arm around him. "I'm here, Lex," he said.

Covington was the neighbor that Elizabeth Campbell had run to for help earlier, asking him to notify the Baquers.

About forty-five minutes passed before the EMS crew was ready to move the shooting victim to the ambulance. A Life-Flight helicopter had set down two blocks away because there was not a large enough landing space at the scene. Baquer watched as his daughter, lying on a backboard, was lifted onto a wheeled stretcher and moved into the ambulance.

Officers cleared a path through the congestion of spectators, and the ambulance inched forward and then sped to the helicopter.

A paramedic approached Baquer and put a hand on his shoulder. "Sir, it appears to be a grazing shot at the side of her head. The pulse is good, her heartbeat is good, but she has lost a lot of blood. She is going to need blood, so you all hurry to Hermann Hospital."

It sounded like an optimistic prognosis, but apparently a second, more deadly gunshot wound had not been discovered because of the victim's blood-matted hair. At the hospital it would be learned that another bullet had smashed into Farah Fratta's brain.

His daughter had been airlifted away only a short time when Baquer spotted a familiar-looking, white-over-yellow Volkswagen pull up and park down the street. He recognized the handsome man who stepped out of the Volks with little Daniel in his arms. The small boy was crying.

The man was Robert Fratta, the estranged husband of the shooting victim.

When he saw him, Baquer exclaimed loudly, "Where the hell has that son-of-a-bitch been? He was supposed to be here with the kids at eight o'clock!"

The angry Baquer started toward Fratta, but was held back by a policeman. A detective who was standing nearby asked Baquer, "Why did you think he was supposed to be here at eight o'clock?"

Because that was the routine, Baquer answered.

Bob Fratta had the children on Wednesday afternoon for visitation and was required to bring them home to their mother no later than 8 P.M., as specified in the visitation agreement.

"That is why Farah was here at eight o'clock, to take the kids when they were brought home," said Baquer. "She always made it a point not to be late.

It was estimated that she had been shot down at about eight o'clock.

Baquer saw a detective approach Fratta and speak briefly with him. Fratta got back in his car.

Baquer and his family left for Hermann Hospital. Taking the wheel of Baquer's car, Covington drove him to the hospital. Betty Baquer rode with their son and daughter-in-law. At the hospital, after locating the emergency room, the family was ushered into a small waiting room.

Baquer recognized David Deitz, a young man who was a close friend of Farah's. He was sitting on the floor, staring. A solemn-faced hospital attendant joined them.

Baquer exclaimed, "I want to see my daughter! Where is she? Please, where is she? Is she alive or dead?"

"I'm sorry, sir. She is dead."

The family members burst into tears. Deitz was sobbing, beating his fists against the wall.

Later, when they were permitted to see her, Farah had been cleaned up. Her father was the first to part the curtain. He could not believe it. His Baby was dead, gone from him forever. Her eyes were half open, seeing nothing. He reached out and tenderly closed her eyes. He bent and kissed her. She felt cold, so cold. He ran from the room. The routine of hospital death moved on slowly and agonizingly. A nurse gave them Farah's personal belongings—a wrist watch and a favorite gold chain with her name, "Farah," etched on it.

While the family was still at the hospital, Covington's wife, Mona, phoned her husband to ask what to do with the Fratta children—Bradley, seven years old, Daniel, five, and Amber, four. Mona said that another neighbor had contacted her, knowing the Covingtons were longtime friends of the Baquers. The neighbor told her that he had been asked by Robert Fratta to keep the children while he went with detectives who wanted to question him. Uncertain when Fratta would return, the neighbor asked Mona if she thought he should put the children to bed at his home for the night. After talking to her husband, Mona Covington told the baby-sitting man that she would keep the children until the Baquers came for them.

When they left the hospital, Covington drove the Baquers to his house. It was early Thursday morning when the bereaved family finally got home. The children had fallen asleep on the way.

Betty Baquer would tell them later on this black day that their mother was dead. She did not sleep the rest of the night. As dawn came, she started slipping into the children's room to see if they were awake. The fourth time that she went in, she found Bradley, the quiet, solemn one of the three, sitting up in bed.

"Hello, Bradley," she said.

The voice of their grandmother awakened Daniel and Amber.

The sleepy Amber asked, "Is my mommy home?" Here it was. She had to tell them now.

"Mommy's gone," she said, her voice catching.

"What do you mean gone, Grandma?" This was from Daniel.

Betty Baquer did not know whether she could continue. She must. The children must be told.

"There was an accident last night. Mommy was killed." Her throat filled and her eyes streamed tears.

"Don't cry, Grandma," Daniel said.

"Who did it?" The startling question came from Bradley.

"We don't know."

Amber's eyes were wide and questioning. "Where is Mommy?"

"She is in the . . . in the home." She did not want to say the "funeral home."

"Can we see Mommy?" Amber asked.

"Yes. We will take all of you to see her later when . . . when she is ready."

She quickly bent to embrace them, hugging them tightly, wetting them with her tears.

Later that day, a female friend of Farah's who had four small children of her own, phoned and asked the grandmother if she wouldn't like her to take the children for the day, this first day without their mother, to feed them and let them play with her children.

Betty Baquer was grateful for the woman's thoughtfulness. She worried about the youngsters being present while visitors were dropping by. She knew it would be a day of tears and grief, and talk about what had happened and why it happened and how and who made it happen.

"I'll bring them back tonight so they can sleep there," the woman said.

"Yes, I want them with us tonight," Betty Baquer said.

It was the first day of a new kind of life for the Baquers, both of whom were nearing retirement, slowing down their lifestyle, putting their later years together into slower gear.

Not now. Now they would be starting all over. Now, having lost a daughter, they would be raising a new generation of children. Lex Baquer would file the court papers seeking the permanent custody of Bradley, Daniel and Amber that day.

The grandparents intended to bring their daughter's two-year legal battle for full custody of the children to a successful conclusion, whatever they had to do.

There was no other way.

Farah Fratta's final hearing to gain permanent custody had only recently been set by the court for November 28, 1994, now less than three weeks away.

Violent death had closed down the mother's relentless fight for her children.

The grandparents were dedicated to finishing the job.

THREE

The fictional detective Sherlock Holmes did his own crime-scene analysis with the help of his handy magnifying glass. Modern investigators know the value of having good crime-scene techs who can make a scene talk to them.

They know that physical evidence when processed by highly trained experts sometimes talks louder and often more accurately than human witnesses.

Harris County Deputy Sheriff J. D. Ferrell and his partner, Deputy Daniel Bloomberg, were crime-scene specialists. They usually worked together as a team. They arrived together at the shooting scene at 10:10 P.M.

Longtime Detective Frank Pratt, assigned to homicide, was the only detective there. He had been at the scene for about five minutes. They talked briefly, but no one knew much at that point: A woman had been shot after she parked her car in the garage. There were three adults who had witnessed part of the shooting from their living room across the street. The victim, a thirty-three-year-old woman named Farah Fratta, apparently had been shot two times after she stepped out of the car. The witnesses across the street said that the shooter, dressed in black, had been picked up by an accomplice driving a small silver car with only one working headlight.

The badly wounded victim, not expected to survive, already had been flown by Life-Flight to the hospital.

Within a short time, word would come from the hospItal that she had died not long after being admitted to the trauma center.

Deputy Constable G. A. Bailey, who patrolled that district of Precinct 4, had been the first officer to respond to the "shooting in progress" report from a 911 dispatcher. He'd secured the scene with yellow crime-scene tape, briefly spoken with the three witnesses and that was about it, Pratt said.

Other detectives from the downtown homicide office of the Harris County Sheriff's Department were on their way.

Ferrell glanced inside the garage and saw the blood on the floor beside the new, light-colored Nissan Maxima where the victim had fallen. Later, detectives would learn the victim had borrowed this car from David Deitz, who had taken Farah Fratta's 1991 Honda Accord to the shop to have the air conditioning worked on. The garage floor was littered with first-aid debris left behind by the EMS people. The two crime-scene officers began making notes and drawings showing the victim's house, garage and a six-foot-high fence that enclosed the backyard. Two small squares in the layout sketch of the backyard showed the locations of a large doghouse and a child's playhouse. The playhouse was big enough for an adult to hide inside.

The two-story brick house fronted west on Forest Fern. The detached garage, which was linked to the house by a breezeway, faced north onto Timber Trails. While examining the fence on the east side of the garage, Ferrell noticed that portions of the wood on top of a gate that faced north toward Timber Trails appeared to be freshly chipped. The raw places on the wood were chipped downward and forward toward the north, and directly below the chipped spots were two deep impressions in the soggy grass that looked like footprints, Ferrell noted. The evidence men believed the shooter—after firing the shots—ran out the garage door where he had entered, jumped on the tall doghouse that was almost next to the gate, stepped over to the gate top and leaped to the ground, leaving his prints in the soggy grass. No shoe tread pattern was visible, but the two impressions definitely were footprints.

Over the next half hour, more homicide investigators arrived. They included Detectives William "Bill" Valerio, Mark Reynolds, Roger Wedgeworth, Larry Davis, and Sergeants Danny Billingsley and John Denholm, who were squad supervisors in the unit. Detectives asked the crime-scene officers to look for any signs that the shooting might have been done during a separate offense such as attempted robbery. Ferrell ruled out that possibility when he examined the victim's black-and-white-striped handbag. It was on the floor on the driver's side toward the rear of the car. The contents of the bag and the purse inside appeared to be undisturbed.

Besides, if robbery had been involved, the gunman easily could have picked up the bag as he fled. There wasn't any evidence that the woman might have interrupted a burglary in progress; both doors to the home were locked and none of the windows showed any signs of a break-in.

A pair of white sneakers and two white socks were on the floor near the left front of the car on the driver's side. The victim had been wearing gym work-out garb, including tennis shoes and socks. The footwear probably had been removed by the medics as they attached emergency medical equipment to her body.

On the floor near the left rear wheel was a set of keys stained with blood, and a single key on a key fob—apparently the car key—was found between the car and the walk-through garage door on the west.

The investigators surmised the victim had the keys in her hand preparing to unlock the back door of her house when she was shot the first time and fell. She had not made it out of the garage to the breezeway leading to the back door. The gunman apparently stepped through the garage door and shot her almost point blank.

To the detectives, the shooting was beginning to look like a planned and cold-blooded hit. The scream after the first shot heard by the neighbors across the street was followed by what probably was a coup de grace shot to finish the job, the detectives believed.

There were blood smears above the car's left, rear door handle and on the left part of the trunk lid, and the left, front side-view mirror was folded upward against the side of the car. Ferrell theorized that the blood smears and bent mirror could be attributed to the medics working in the narrow space between the car and west garage wall.

Searching the scene for ballistic evidence, Ferrell was scanning the south, back wall of the garage when he noticed a child's toy life preserver hanging about six feet above the floor, almost at eye-level for him.

What caught his attention was a nick, or some kind

of breach, in the material at the top of the water toy. Ferrell probed in that spot and was rewarded by finding the spent fragment of a bullet.

He found another spent bullet fragment on the floor, roughly three feet southwest of the left rear end of the car. No weapon was found, but if and when one did turn up, the detectives now had two fragments that could be compared to bullets test fired from the gun.

Ferrell and his partner dusted the interior and exterior of the car for possible latent fingerprints, as well as the outside entry doors to the house and the walk-through door at the side of the garage. Numerous photos of the crime scene were taken under the supervision of the crime-scene officer.

After Lex Baquer had noticed Robert Fratta's arrival, it was Constable Bailey who had the first conversation with the estranged husband. When Fratta got out of his Volkswagen and started toward two detectives who were talking together, the constable intercepted him.

Fratta said he wanted to talk to the detectives. The constable told him to "hold up for a little bit because the detectives are busy."

Fratta said, "Tell them to expedite it, will you, because I've got my kids with me. I'm in a hurry."

The constable notified one of the detectives of Fratta's presence. The detective went over to Fratta and instructed him to wait in his car, it would be a few minutes. When Detective William Valerio showed up, Constable Bailey informed him that the estranged husband was wanting to talk to someone.

Bailey gestured toward a good-looking man with an

excellent physique, wearing blue jeans, a striped polo shirt with no collar and cowboy boots. He was lounging with his back against the side of the Volkswagen, which was parked in front of the Fratta home on Forest Fern.

Before approaching Fratta, Valerio looked over the scene for a few minutes and was briefed by Detective Pratt on what had been learned so far.

Then he walked over to Bob Fratta.

The first thing that struck Valerio about the estranged husband was the man's composure and his lack of any visible emotion about the shooting attack on his wife. Fratta appeared to be "well in command" of the situation, as the detective later would describe the husband's appearance.

Valerio introduced himself and asked Fratta several routine questions: Where he had been earlier and when did he arrive here. Fratta said he had taken his children earlier in the evening to a catechism class and a church service at a Catholic church and then had driven here to return them to their mother. It was about 9 P.M. when he got here.

Fratta gestured toward the three children in his car and said he wanted to get them to the hospital to see their mother before she died. His cool and relaxed, matter-of-fact manner continued to puzzle the detective. The detective said it would not be likely that any family member could see the gravely wounded mother while the trauma team was fighting to save her life.

Valerio asked Fratta if he would accompany him to the homicide office to make a statement, since conditions at the scene would make their talking difficult.

Fratta said he would, but there was the matter of his kids in the car.

"Is there someone out here you know who could keep them until we are through?" Valerio asked.

Fratta mentioned a neighbor who lived in the house north of the Fratta home. He recalled his wife previously had employed a teenage girl at that address as a baby-sitter.

Valerio and Fratta went to the residence, and the father of the former baby-sitter agreed to keep the children while Fratta went with the officer. That settled, Valerio asked Fratta to follow him in his own vehicle to the homicide office on Lockwood in downtown Houston.

He emphasized that Fratta was not under arrest and any statement he might give would be voluntary on his part.

The detective, with Fratta right behind him, turned into the homicide office parking lot about 11:20 P.M. and they entered the large building that some people have said looks like a warehouse from the outside.

They went upstairs to the homicide office. Valerio ushered Fratta into an interview room, where their conversation would be recorded and also would be filmed by a camera concealed in the ceiling.

During the nearly two-hour interrogation, Fratta maintained his calm, patient and unemotional demeanor. He said that he was a police officer himself, a public safety officer at the nearby town of Missouri City, Texas. He obviously was familiar with police procedures.

Fratta related that Wednesday was the day he had a court-approved visitation with his children. He said he had previously made arrangements with their mother to take Bradley, the oldest boy, to a Catholic church class. There was a church nursery for the younger children.

After picking them up that afternoon at their school, Fratta had driven them by his own house to feed four pets—a boa python, an iguana, a dog and a cat.

Valerio thought to himself that it sounded like a zoo.

Fratta said he then took the youngsters to a Wyatt's Cafeteria, one of their favorite eating places, and bought them dinner. From there they drove to the St. Mary's Catholic Church on South Houston in Humble, where Bradley was to have his final catechism class. Fratta remained at the church while his boy went to the class.

Fratta recalled they had not left the church until shortly after 8:30 P.M. He said they stopped at Fratta's house briefly, then started for Farah Fratta's home. On the way, they stopped at a convenience store where the children bought some bubble gum.

Minutes later they arrived at the children's home to be greeted by pandemonium—police cars, police officers and people and vehicles clogging the street.

It would all need checking, Valerio thought, but it looked as if Bob Fratta had himself a good alibi for the time period in which his wife was shot by a stalking gunman. At least, he wasn't the shooter, the detective thought. But in the detective's opinion, that did not eliminate him from being involved.

During the questioning, Fratta displayed intense hostility toward his wife and readily admitted that he disliked her and had fought with her bitterly for two years in their divorce-custody dispute. He thought he was being treated unfairly by her and the courts. But his anger toward her did not mean that he wanted her dead, the estranged husband said.

He said that the final hearing to determine which parent would have permanent custody of the children was coming up on November 28, not quite three weeks off.

During the interview, Valerio noticed that Fratta's pager went off a couple of times. Fratta asked if he could return the calls, and he was permitted to use a phone at a desk in one of the detectives' empty cubicles. Valerio did not try to listen in on the calls or to find out what numbers Fratta called.

Fratta agreed to give a written statement on what had been covered in the oral interview, and when that was completed, Valerio asked him if he would sign a consent-to-search form to allow the detective to search the Volkswagen. Fratta agreed and signed the form that Valerio filled out.

Fratta handed over the car keys. Out in the parking lot, Valerio opened the driver's side door of the Volkswagen and shined his flashlight over the interior. Nothing of interest. He snapped a photo with a Polaroid camera.

He used a smaller key to open the glove compartment. Inside he saw a 9-mm. pistol. Nothing unusual about that, the guy had said he was a police officer in Missouri City. There also was a white envelope. No writing or markings on it. He snapped a photograph of the compartment's contents, then took out the envelope and looked inside.

Currency, several bills. He counted $1,050 in cash. There was no bank deposit slip, or anything that showed what the money might be for. Nobody usually carried that much cash around in an envelope, Valerio thought, unless intending to do something with it pretty quickly.

The thought crossed his mind: Could it be payoff money for a hired killer?

The detective counted the money: Five $100 bills, twenty-five $20 bills and one $50 bill. Not much of a payoff, if that was what it was intended for. The detective didn't think murder-for-hire came that cheap.

Valerio opened the car's trunk. It contained the usual stuff in a car trunk, but two items caught his interest. One was a personal address book of Fratta's with phone numbers and other data written beside the names, many of them women's names. The other item was a personal diary of Fratta's.

Returning to the office, Valerio asked about the envelope of cash.

"Forget to make your bank deposit? That's quite a bit of cash to leave laying around in a glove compartment."

Fratta said the cash was for paying a man for some carpet work done in Fratta's house. He had thought he might see the carpet worker this evening or tomorrow.

During the remainder of the night and on into the next day, Fratta was questioned in relays by Valerio and other homicide detectives. Though Fratta answered many of the questions, the investigators came up with zip. His demeanor remained one of calmness during the long interrogation.

Valerio's gut feeling was that this fellow cop was being deceptive, to put it mildly.

Undoubtedly, Fratta had an alibi for his whereabouts at the time of the shooting—the class for his son that he said he attended. There would be plenty of witnesses who could verify his story. Valerio knew that.

But his cop's instincts told him that that did not mean that Bob Fratta was not involved up to his muscular neck in the murder of his wife.

Valerio and the other detectives were beginning to think "hit job"—that Farah Fratta had been shot and killed by a paid gunman. The fact that the shooter had been picked up by an accomplice in a car pointed to an organized plot.

But at this point the homicide men were far away from proving anything.

Bob Fratta walked out of the homicide office a weary but free man on midafternoon Thursday, after spending some fourteen or fifteen hours being grilled.

As the suspect started out the door, Sergeant John Denholm said, "Hey, Fratta, you forgot your car keys." Disgruntled by Fratta's lack of cooperation and smugness, Denholm threw the keys toward Fratta, harder than he meant to. Fratta tried to catch them, but they went through his hands and struck him on the cheek, drawing blood.

He appeared to be squeezing the slightly bleeding scratch on his face. Obviously he was making the most of it before the mob of eager print and electronic reporters and photographers. The media people were surprised by Fratta's response. He did not try to avoid them and get away as quickly as possible. He appeared to almost bask in the limelight, at least in the minds of veteran news gatherers recalling how countless other suspects had reacted in the past. The reporters couldn't believe it. The smirking Fratta smiled often as he answered questions, even laughed. It was all there on the evening newscasts.

"It's extremely rough," Fratta said. "I mean, I fully understand why I'm their main suspect, but this makes a tough time a lot tougher. All I can do right now is hope they find who did it. Then this part of my ordeal will be over. I haven't even had a chance to talk to my kids yet. I was there [in the homicide office] all day."

Fratta had held the impromptu press conference immediately after emerging from the door of the homicide headquarters. He started walking to his car, but stopped again for more questions before getting into his vehicle.

Sergeant Denholm minced no words when he spoke to reporters a short time later. After the hours that he and the other detectives had spent with Fratta, Denholm was plainly a disgusted and frustrated policeman over what he considered plain old stonewalling by Fratta. The veteran homicide detective said Fratta refused to cooperate with detectives in the case. "He's just been real amused by this whole thing," Denholm said.

In another part of the Houston area that evening, in the little town of Humble not many miles from where Farah Fratta had been slain the day before, a big man with a muscular build and wearing glasses sat with his pretty girlfriend in her apartment watching the six o'clock news. They had seen Bob Fratta's homicide parking lot chat with the press.

"Bob better quit doing all that smirking and laughing on TV," the man said.

His luscious-looking girlfriend nodded, but said

nothing. She had her own haunting secrets that, if known to the man with her, would immediatcly place her in peril of her very life.

Inwardly, she shuddered.

FOUR

When he first got the call to assist in a shooting investigation on Forest Fern in Atascocita that Wednesday in November, homicide Detective Larry Davis thought the address was familiar. When he pulled up at the two-story brick home it all came back to him.

It had been less than four months ago, in late June 1994, that he had been assigned to investigate a home invasion case at this house. He remembered that the complainant was a pretty woman named Farah Fratta.

The Harris County Constable's Office, Precinct 4, made the first response to a 911 call from a hysterical woman reporting she had been attacked by an intruder wearing a black ski mask. She was in such an emotional state that it was difficult to understand her. The call for help came shortly after 4 A.M.

Farah Fratta was awakened in her upstairs bedroom by a sound. Her bedroom door was open. The air conditioning was on high because of the blazing summer heat that enveloped the southeast Texas coastal area that time of year. The noise had sounded like the ruffle of window blinds. Suddenly a big man in a black ski mask was standing beside her bed. She screamed and sat up.

Her piercing shriek awakened her son, Daniel, who was sleeping with her. The boy sat up too.

The man in the ski mask asked brusquely, "Who's that?"

"That's my son," she said, her voice reflecting the terror that gripped her.

"I've come to talk about Bob," the intruder said. He was holding a small black object that resembled an electric razor and also carrying a bottle of tequila.

The oldest boy, Bradley, had been sleeping downstairs on the living room couch and little Amber was slumbering in her room upstairs, a night monitor near her bed linking the room to her mother's.

At the loud scream, the tiny girl ran down the stairway crying, "Mommy! Mommy!" Bradley also came into the room. All of them were crying now.

"Whatever you are going to do, don't do it in front of my children, please!" the terrified mother sobbed.

The man roughly pushed all three children out the door and closed it. They pounded on the door and continued to cry and scream.

The masked man turned around and ordered her, "Turn over!" He grabbed her by one of her heels and jerked her around in the bed. He pulled down one shoulder strap of her nightgown, jabbed the black object against her shoulder and she screamed in intense pain as electricity surged between the two prongs on the object.

From the victim's description, detectives later would identify the instrument of torture as a stun gun, a hand-held, battery-operated device that delivers a powerful electrical shock upon contact. It is commonly used by police officers and often carried by citizens, especially women, as a defensive weapon.

When triggered, the stun gun crackles and its jolt is like a small lightning bolt.

The menacing masked man again pressed the horrible black thing against her throat, producing another piercing scream as her skin was seared by the electrical charge. It left the smell of scorched skin. The sobbing and screaming children continued to pound on the door, their actions urgent now at the sound of their mother's screams.

Just as quickly as he had appeared, the torturer fled, grabbing Farah's portable telephone from a table to prevent her from calling the police. He had overlooked another phone, which she used.

A patrol officer from the constable's office responded within minutes and took the initial report; the victim declined the patrolman's offer to take her somewhere for examination and treatment of the electrical burns.

Later, Sergeant Robert Johnson, making a followup call about 7 A.M. on the report made by one of his patrol officers, noted that the young woman had red burn marks on her throat and shoulder and was still frightened out of her wits.

In their examination of the house to find out how the stun-gun terrorist had gotten inside, the officers discovered a small hole in a rear window next to the sliding patio door. There were glass shavings below the hole.

The investigators believed the intruder had used a battery-operated hand drill to make the tiny hole, through which a slender object had been inserted to open the door mechanism.

Besides being ruthless and sadistic, the intruder obviously was a professional break-in artist who knew his business. But they found no clues that might help identify him.

Farah Fratta described him as tall and muscular, bigger than her estranged husband with whom she was involved in a lengthy and bitter divorce and custody fight. She thought the phantom night prowler was wearing glasses underneath the ski mask. She did not recognize his voice, saying only it was both threatening and controlled, but that it definitely was not her husband's voice.

She told Detective Davis when he questioned her that for the burglar to have been her husband, Bob Fratta, the glasses he wore and his voice would have had to be faked.

Lex Baquer answered the phone at 8 A.M.

Calling was his daughter, Farah, sounding calm and self-possessed.

"Dad, don't panic," she said. "I'm going to tell you something."

Sensing the tightness in her speech, Baquer said, "What is it, Baby? What's the matter?"

She quietly related the details of her ordeal at the hands of an unknown, masked assailant. "I was absolutely scared to death, Dad. I was afraid he would hurt the children. I'm okay," she added quickly. "Just awfully shook up. I feel like I'm being stalked, and I don't really know why, unless it has something to do with Bob and the custody case. I don't know what to do." She had become tearful.

Baquer drove at high speed to his daughter's home to offer comfort and make plans and initiate procedures to prevent another act of terrorism. He strongly felt that his son-of-a-bitch of a son-in-law had done it, or was involved some way.

Constable and sheriff investigators were still at the house when he got there. They were taking pictures of the window and the small hole that had been drilled. Photographs also were made of the electric burns on Farah's throat and shoulder.

"His build was like Bob's, he even walked like him, but he was a bigger man than Bob," the attack victim recalled. "I have never heard his voice before. I know it was not Bob's voice. And he had on glasses under the mask."

Farah Fratta and her children moved in with her parents. Extra police patrols were arranged.

But there was no further harassment of a violent nature. Still, Farah was so nervous and apprehensive that she could barely work at her job as an airline clerk, one that required vitality and personality to deal successfully with customers who sometimes were on edge themselves.

Finally, after three weeks, she said to her father, "Dad, I have to go back. I can't live like this. I have to go back to my home."

Baquer took all possible precautions. An alarm system was installed, his daughter was equipped with a panic button that hung around her neck and local patrol officers were asked to keep watch and check her residence regularly.

Nothing more happened and a sense of normalcy returned to both family's households.

No arrests were made in the June 28, 1994, episode. It was an unsolved case.

But Bob Fratta was making life miserable for his separated wife, stalking her in small and subtle ways. Even his voice on the phone filled her with fear.

While she was at work, he would come to her house and take things from the garage. He did not try to enter the house because the newly installed alarm system was always on. If set off, it would bring a bunch of cops in a matter of minutes.

Then came the brutal murder by a man who also was wearing black clothing.

Homicide detectives had no doubt that the torture episode and the shooting death were related. They believed Bob Fratta was involved in both cases. Proving their theory and nailing a suspect was another thing.

Fratta was still employed on his job as a public safety officer at Missouri City. The job was one which combined fireman and policeman duties, a personnel alternative often chosen by smaller towns.

Fratta's friends and fellow employees felt he did a good, professional job, though he did draw temporary probation twice—once for alleged sexual harassment of a woman employee and again for insubordination.

Some colleagues even felt sorry for him, thinking that he was being mistreated by his wife and the courts by the amount of the court-imposed child support. Especially other firemen who had had wife troubles were Fratta sympathizers.

FIVE

The scatological and masochistic sexual appetites of Bob Fratta did not surface, publicly at least, until his lawyer asked beautiful Farah Fratta a pointed question while taking her deposition during a bitterly fought child custody fight that started in 1992. Lawyers take depositions to prepare for the eventual trial.

Present in the law office that December 15, 1993, for the deposition taking were Farah, her attorney, Bob Fratta, his attorney and a court reporter.

The divorce case had been filed in March 1992 by Farah's lawyer as a so-called "fault divorce." The majority of divorce suits in Texas, those that are uncontested, are filed without a "fault" clause. In those relatively peaceful cases the marriage property is divided on a fifty-fifty basis.

A fault divorce is one in which the parties have not agreed on the half-and-half property settlement, or anything else, and the offended party as determined by a court trial will gain more than the fifty percent, much more in some cases.

In the filing of Farah Fratta's case as a fault divorce, the petition alleged the fault of "cruelty" without stating any specifics. Farah's lawyer was saving those specifics as a legal bombshell for the trial.

During the deposition questioning of the wife, Bob Fratta's attorney looking at the fault allegation of cruelty, asked her, "How would you define cruelty?"

The question opened the door for an unsuspected answer by the soft-spoken wife, and later a sickeningly detailed follow-up psychological report on Bob Fratta's sexual preferences that would prompt the presiding family court judge to state that in twenty-three years of family-oriented legal work he had "never heard this degree of depravity . . . and bizarre sexual behavior."

Farah Fratta turned to the attorney and answered that her definition of cruelty was her husband's revolting sexual requests: He wanted her to defecate in his mouth, urinate on his face, and choke him and hit him in the stomach while he was masturbating, among other of his outrageously deviant sexual activities.

The dark secrets of the sexual abuse that she had been too ashamed to tell anyone were out in the open now.

But the humiliating revelations about Bob Fratta's twisted sexual nature sealed her doom.

In its early years, their marriage seemingly had been a happy one. The events leading to the marriage of Farah Baquer and Robert Alan Fratta began in 1981 when Lex Baquer moved his family from London, England, to America.

Baquer had visited America several times, and he loved the enterprising country and its opportunities.

During one of those trips, he called his family from Ohio in January 1981. At that time, his wife, Betty, daughter, Farah, and son, Zain, all had jobs in London.

He talked to each of them about moving to America, his enthusiasm showing through.

To his wife, he explained with excitement in his voice, "This is what I want to do, honey. Since I don't have a business in London, and the taxes are so high, and people are getting a bit too crowded, I want to try my hand in America."

Betty Baquer was not enthusiastic about the move, but was agreeable.

"I don't mind, but I don't want to live in Ohio—it's too cold," she said. That suited Lex just fine.

"Look, honey, you've heard me say it many times. I always wanted to live in Texas. I have always had a desire for the open country. Sunshine, warm weather, bright stars, sleeping outside in a tent, camping, horse riding. I used to ride horses when I was young. My father had lots of horses. Doesn't that sound grand?"

From boyhood he was a big fan of movies about Texas. He had even seen one or two in which reasonably wealthy Englishmen had come to Texas, bought ranches and became cattle-baron millionaires.

Lex had made his latest trip to the United States when his brother-in-law in Ohio died after a heart operation.

He also had spent time with his brother in Boston, Massachusetts. Baquer had stayed on in Ohio for a while to help his sister with probating the will and other matters.

As part of the move to a new land, Baquer wanted his son, Zain, to join him in an automobile-repair garage and automatic-transmission business.

"How about you joining me?" the father asked when his son came on the phone. "With your mechanical ability and my business ability and marketing experience, we will make a go of it."

"I'm game, Dad," Zain said.

But his daughter, Farah, was opposed to the drastic change. She was born outside London in lovely Guilford Survey on August 5, 1961. She now was a pretty young lady of nineteen, had many friends from all the way back to early school days, including the young man she was engaged to marry.

After graduation from John Newman High School at Croydon Surrey, near London, she had enrolled in college, taking courses to qualify her as a travel agent. She was working at that job in London.

Far and above some of her more routine reasons for not wanting to leave England, was her engagement to the man that even her protective dad approved of wholeheartedly.

Give all this up for the foreign land of America where she knew no one, a land so far different in culture and lifestyle from London and the beautiful English countryside where she grew up? Go to the United States? Never!

Life in her small town that had only one street, called High Street, was serene and full of fun and longtime and dear friends. The tiny hamlet boasted two or three little shops, two cinemas, a large hospital, three small banks, two elementary schools, two high schools and not much more except those awfully wonderful people and the oh-so-pretty environment in which they lived.

When she expressed her reluctance to leave these happy surroundings, her father said, "Look, Baby. Just give yourself a chance, a month say, and if you don't like it, you can always go back and live with your grandmother. And that holds true for all of us. We can always go back."

Farah had a close relationship with her grandmother and, at nineteen, she was an adult who could have her own life. She guessed that the "give it a try" plan of her father's sounded feasible, especially his assurance that "You can always go back."

She loved her dad for everything he was—a caring father always emphasizing to his children high standards and the values of family life, as they had been taught and handed down generation by generation in his own family. He liked to tell everybody that there had never been a divorce in his family, down through the ages.

Lex and Betty Baquer had lived in England since 1958. Before that, they traveled and lived in other parts of the world, mainly the Far East, where Baquer had family connections.

When his daughter was about three, Baquer took a job with a British corporation in the Far East. He worked for the British firm for six years.

While they were there, Farah attended an English-speaking school in Bangladesh, which was then East Pakistan. They had returned to England in 1964.

There Farah finished her schooling, and it was in high school that she met and dated the youth who was her fiancé. Her dad had liked him from the moment he met the young man.

Farah was a popular student. She excelled in sewing and baking and was active in sports—hockey and tennis and the swimming team. She was a studious girl and enjoyed reading.

Early on, she had decided to be a travel agent, and she took courses in high school and during eighteen months of college that would be helpful in that career. She was very good at geography and she loved to travel.

From the time she was a school girl and on into her adult years, she baked a chocolate cake, his favorite, for her dad every week. She did not smoke or drink. She enjoyed socializing with her friends. She liked to dance. She loved animals.

When she began dating, her parents set strict curfews, and she and her boyfriends always observed them. Her father told her dates that if they came home one minute late, it was the end of their going out with Farah.

Baquer flew back to London in February, 1981, and made all the arrangements for his family to join him in the United States. In the middle of March 1981, the Baquers flew to the U.S., stopping first in Boston to pick up the car that Baquer had purchased from his sister in Ohio after her husband's death. Before going for his family, he had left the car with his Massachusetts brother.

They stopped to visit the Ohio sister, disregarding warnings by his "northern" relatives that he would not like Texas.

"I'm going to slow down my life a bit," said Baquer. "And I like Texas. I am going to Texas and see what I can find."

They drove straight through to Texas, entering the state by Texarkana and then making what was intended as a night stopover in Humble, Texas, to take a look at the nearby booming city of Houston. The date was March 31, 1981.

They immediately liked Humble as a place to live. They were fascinated by how far they could see across the sweeping plains, cherished the warm days and the friendliness of the people. Lex "spread his wings," as he put it, and quickly made business contacts, secured loans from the local bank, bought a house and set up the father-son automatic-transmission shop.

The British family soon became popular residents of the town. Baquer made it a point to get acquainted with all of the local officials. He joined the Chamber of Commerce.

His newly opened business did well. His customers appreciated the good service, integrity and honesty offered by Baquer and his son.

Life wasn't so easy for his daughter, Farah. Baquer was sad to see that she cried frequently. Almost for a month the tears flowed. Her fiancé came twice to visit her, and she flew back to London one time.

Before another trip to London, the Baquers suggested that it wouldn't hurt for Farah to place her resumé with some airlines, even though she was looking for a job as a travel agent. She gave her resumé to British Airways and American Airlines.

She said after a visit to Houston's busy International Airport that she would prefer having a job with British Airways because life there was at a slower pace, nothing like the hurlyburly of the American Airline ticket counters. She still liked the British way of doing things.

But the first job offer she received was from American. The airline had an opening for a temporary ticket agent. It was an auxiliary type of job. When the ticket lines were long and time was running short to meet flight schedules, Farah's job as temporary clerk was to go out among the customers in line and transact business to ease the pressure at the ticket counters. She was a travel agent at last.

She was exceptionally good at the roving agent duties, flashing the smile and friendly personality that were well received by harried passengers. Before long she was working as a permanent ticket agent behind the counter.

That was where she met a handsome, charming senior ticket agent named Robert Fratta. He had the physique of a Greek god. He said he was a dedicated body-building "freak." In every way he was a charmer. He didn't seem to mind or worry that she already was wearing a large diamond engagement ring.

The two together in their ticket agent uniforms looked like something out of a popular magazine advertisement.

Farah Baquer was overwhelmed by everything about Bob Fratta. Even when several of the women agents who had dated Fratta told her, "Beware of this guy," she put it down to maybe jealousy on the part of former and rejected girlfriends.

Bob Fratta was what some of the girls called "brassy." Obviously he had a big ego, but at the same time he was charming. Farah thought this American Prince Charming was "very sweet," even well-liked by his male colleagues, who were more than a little envious of his good looks and muscular but well-honed physique. He was good at the counter, too, handling the ticket lines fast and easily cajoling impatient or upset customers. They would show up grouchy and complaining and go away with a big smile.

Bob Fratta had the golden touch with people, but especially with women, young and old. He was the lover they had dreamed of or the son they had always wanted.

* * *

Baquer noticed that his daughter was on the phone for long stretches of time. It seemed like whenever he wanted to make a call, the phone was tied up. She said she was talking to one of her friends, another ticket agent. One day after she hung up from a drawn-out conversation, Baquer said, "Look, if you want to talk to your friend, you're earning money now. You should get your own telephone."

She did.

Another time, Baquer happened to walk by his daughter's room when the door was partly ajar, and he could hear her talking on the phone. He noticed that she had the cover over her head while she talked.

At the first opportunity, he asked, "Who's this guy you are talking to all the time, Baby? And under the covers at that."

She blushed slightly. "How do you know it's a guy?"

"Come on, honey. I'm your dad."

She told him that his name was Bob Fratta.

"What's his background?" She was used to that question.

"Well, he's Italian and he's from New York."

"Is he married?" The protective dad was at it again.

"No, Daddy, he's single. He's really awfully nice and polite and good looking and smart, and he seems to like me a lot, Dad."

Baquer backed off a little. "I hope you don't mind my asking, Baby, but I like to know who my daughter is involved with. And you know my attitude. I don't care who you are going out with, but I still want to know who you are going out with."

Farah smiled before she answered. "He comes from a small New York town named Westbury on Long Island. I have never met his mother, and he has a sister. She works at a bank, and is pretty much a loan officer or something, a real nice person. And his father is dead."

She said Fratta was a little older than she was and had never been married. He was a college graduate. He was well liked on the job and had a high performance rating.

"Well, at least it sounds like you're thinking. Baby, I would like you to bring this young man home, I would like to meet him. Because I like to know who he is."

"Okay, Dad. You will meet him."

One evening she brought Bob Fratta home to meet her family. Baquer was impressed at first sight: He was a nice-looking guy, he observed, fair, light hair, blue eyes, a mustache, well built—it was obvious he was a bodybuilder.

He liked the mustache because Baquer and all the men in his family wore a mustache. Fratta's was neatly trimmed, and he had good white teeth under it.

He spoke easily and personably and smiled a lot. He had a good, solid handshake. And he presented himself like a gentleman—"Yes, sir" and all that. Baquer accepted him as a gentleman, even if he didn't really know much about the man.

Fratta and Farah began dating regularly. Twice Lex and his wife went out with them. They had a pleasant time. Zain Baquer never associated with Fratta. It was plain that, for some reason which he never mentioned, he did not like him. Zain kept his distance. He tolerated Fratta because his sister liked him so much. As the days passed, Baquer could see that his daughter liked this man very much. Probably loved him, from all appearances.

Late one evening when she came home from a date, he said, "Farah, you two are very close. Anyone can see that. Are you serious about this guy?"

She said, "Yes, I am, Dad, very serious."

"Not fair. You are wearing a diamond engagement ring from that boy in London. That poor guy must still be paying for that diamond ring. You should write him a letter and tell him what's going on. You should be fair about this. You know, life is not so easy in London. Not as good as in America. You should tell him what's going on."

His daughter wrote a letter to her English fiancé. She had it in her hand, and she said, "Do you want to read it, Dad?"

"No, I am sure you have written a very appropriate letter."

She told him anyway, that she had written that they both were still very young. "I think we should give ourselves an opportunity to go our different ways, and if we still have a strong feeling for each other, we can get back together. Right now I am seeing another guy."

Not long afterward, Farah received an answer. Surprisingly, he said about the same thing that she had written. He was also seeing another young woman. His letter said, "Yes, I don't mind, but I love you very much. But I think you also want to give me the opportunity to look around, as you say."

Farah wrote him again. She mentioned that when her father had learned that she was getting serious about another man, he had said that it was not fair to her fiancé, and she should send the engagement ring back. She was mailing it to her grandmother, who would call him when the ring arrived. She was free to marry Bob Fratta now.

Fate had dropped the axe.

SIX

The next eighteen months were happy ones for Farah Baquer. She and Bob Fratta were dating regularly. She also was getting promotion after promotion with the airline. One day she announced to her father that she and Fratta were going to get married.

"Bob wants to talk to you," she told her father.

That was a good start for the young man, Baquer thought.

It was wintertime and cold enough even in Humble, Texas, for a fire in the fireplace. The Baquers, their daughter and Fratta were sitting around the fire when Fratta stood up and walked over to Baquer.

"Sir, I would like to have your daughter's hand in marriage," he said. Baquer couldn't believe his ears—the formality of the statement. Not the American approach at all. He wouldn't have been surprised to hear him say, "Hey, old man, I want to marry your daughter." Looking back later, Baquer decided his future son-in-law must have done his homework, probably had asked Farah what her father might expect in the situation and had been well briefed.

Undoubtedly, Fratta had done his homework on British manners.

Baquer only nodded, shaking hands, trying to keep

back the tears. "Are you two in love? You know, she is my only girl, and she's very precious to me. She's my baby. She's grown up, but she's still my baby to me."

Still heavy on the "sir," Fratta vowed he would take good care of her. He had already bought her a large diamond engagement ring. Betty Baquer was reserved in her reaction to the marriage plans. "I just want her to be happy," she said later to her husband.

They were married on May 7, 1983. It was a small wedding, as weddings go. Farah chose her brides-maids from her friends at the office. Fratta's sister came down from New York and was one of the bridesmaids. Zain was dating an English girl, who came from London for the event. The Frattas were Catholics, although Fratta himself was not known to attend church services often, if at all. The wedding took place in a Catholic church in Humble, followed by a reception in the church annex.

A few weeks after the wedding, Bob Fratta decided to resign his job with American Airlines to take advantage of a "golden handshake," a downsizing plan by the airline to cut back its workforce by offering a $10,000 resignation incentive. Fratta liked the idea and he took the $10,000 lump sum.

But now he was without a job and another didn't seem to be in the offing. Baquer thought it was a dumb decision to leave a good-paying job without lining up another one. Still, when Fratta asked about going into the transmission business with his father-in-law, Baquer agreed. They both put up $2,000. Baquer ordered an inventory of parts from a supplier. They called the transmission sales business Baquer & Fratta Co.

"But it never got off the ground," Baquer would

later recall. "For the simple reason Bob was never there early in the morning. He was never a worker." He told his son-in-law it was not going to work, and they dissolved the partnership. It was the first indication to his father-in-law that Fratta was a slacker, always looking for a way to make big "easy" money instead of holding a regular job.

Farah continued to work for the airline. Fortunately she was earning a good salary, because Fratta's exodus payoff had been depleted long before he was working again.

Fratta had a friend who was a public safety officer, a combination fireman-policeman, for Missouri City, near Houston. Fratta decided to attend the training school for firefighters at Texas A & M and obtain the state license necessary to be a fireman. His wife worked extra shifts to pay his way through the training school. He first landed a job as a firefighter in Conroe, Texas, and about a year later got the job he wanted at Missouri City. The couple had bought a house in the Conroe area.

When Farah learned she was pregnant, she wanted to move closer to her parents. They moved into the house on Forest Fern in Atascocita, where Bradley was born on December 16, 1986. When it happened, one of the first things Farah did was phone Lex Baquer. "Dad, you're a grandfather," she said.

The Frattas had joined the President and First Lady Spa, a popular workout gym in Humble. They introduced Baquer to the fitness routines of the spa's health club. Baquer knew that his son-in-law was a fanatic about keeping his body in top shape. Fratta often expressed his ambition to be selected Mr. Texas, the bodybuilder champ of the state. He liked to show off his trim and muscular physique. Once at a beach party where the coolness of the day had some of the people talking about calling it quits to the outing, Fratta had already doffed his pullover shirt to better display his brawny chest. Whatever the occasion, he was always the center of admiration of the women present.

Baquer knew that his son-in-law, in addition to his rigid gym workout regimen, used steroids to help mold the muscles. He had heard this from Farah, who downplayed it as nothing to worry about—Bob said they were prescribed by doctors.

About a year after Bradley was born, another baby was on the way. But before she became pregnant, Baquer had noticed that Farah was not her usual, buoyant self. She said nothing was wrong and always smiled that smile of hers, but she was looking run-down.

If there was a problem, she was trying to solve it herself, her father decided. She knew that he had a bad temper, and that might be why she was keeping her own council, Baquer thought.

One time when he encountered Bob Fratta at the gym, Baquer was candid about his concern with Farah's tense and deteriorating appearance, and he said, "Bob, tell me, is there something wrong at home? Are Farah and you having a problem?"

"Oh, that's her imagination, Lex. Nothing is wrong. Everything is perfect. She'll be fine when the baby is born."

Baquer was in the kitchen washing the few dishes from a quick meal when through the window he saw Farah pull up in her car and get out with little Daniel. He had been born on July 4, 1988, and at five months, he was already a little charmer. Instead of coming into the house, she sat down on the lawn with Daniel. Baquer went outside to play with his newest grandson. Farah was low in mood again, without much to say.

Baquer went back inside. His wife was on her way out.

"Betty, see if you can find out what is going on." He felt that Betty probably knew more than she was telling him. He thought that women found it easier to talk about these things among themselves.

"There's a problem." That's all his wife said. She wasn't going to talk about it, either, if indeed she knew something.

"Well, is it a husband and wife problem? Please, let me know if it is anything serious."

"No, there's nothing." She turned her face from him and went outside to join Farah and Daniel.

Maybe he was imagining things. It was easy to do, when he thought there might be something going on that was making his baby unhappy.

Then their daughter came by the Baquers' house one morning to break the bad news. She and Bob were splitting up.

"I asked him to leave. I don't want to talk about it, Dad. Maybe we can work it out if we're not together for a while."

The separation lasted only a month, and Farah took him back. She still did not want to discuss what kind of trouble they were having. "We just separated, that's all," she said. Looking back, Baquer believed the trouble between them had started before Daniel was born. He wondered if she had had another baby hoping to restore the marital relationship that for some unknown reason had soured badly.

But he sensed things were no better between them, even though they were living together again.

At the gym he struck up a conversation with his son-in-law. "Bob, I don't like to interfere in my daughter's life. I have always let my children work out their problems, unless they ask me to help. Farah has not said anything, but I know something is wrong."

Fratta frowned. "Nothing, there's nothing. I don't know what your daughter is making such a big deal about. She has nothing to cry about. It's your daughter who is bringing all this on."

"Okay, I'll talk to her," Baquer said.

He had lunch with Farah two or three times, hoping to find out what was wrong, to find some way to clear the troubled domestic waters. Farah was not budging from her previous attitude of silence.

But a few weeks later she had some startling news for her parents.

"I'm pregnant," she said quietly. Her softly spoken words might as well have been an earthshaking blast of thunder as far as the effect they had on her father.

He started to say, "Farah, with all the problems . . ." But he stopped before finishing the sentence.

"It was a mistake," she said.

After she left, Baquer turned to his wife. "Betty, what the hell is this? Here she has told me several times that she wants a divorce. And she goes and gets pregnant again."

It was driving him nuts. He could not stand to see his daughter this unhappy, her sad aloneness, her reluctance to seek help from him or anyone else who was trying to make sense of her stubborn "stand-alone" mind-set.

And now she was pregnant again!

Was she, he wondered, thinking like so many women do in this unhappy situation: Where would I go? What would I do about the children? The children would grow up without a father. And she must be thinking of those ingrained family values from her strict upbringing: "Never a divorce in the history of our family. . . . Thirteen brothers and sisters in our family, all married only one time, no divorces, no start-overs with somebody else." And she knew, too, that Bradley looked up to his father as a hero, too young to know that his father was brainwashing him.

On May 26, 1990, a baby girl was born. They named her Amber Nicole. She was a beautiful baby.

In October 1991, the Frattas and their three children, accompanied by Bob's sister, took a vacation in Maine. It was a gusty day and they were traveling on an interstate with the sister driving the van. Bob was in the passenger seat beside her, Farah was in the middle seat with Amber at her left. Bradley and Daniel were in the backseat.

Suddenly the van began swerving. Bob's sister was trying to bring it under control when it flipped.

Fratta realized that he was dangling upside down by his seat belt, and he heard the children screaming and crying. Although he had suffered a severe concussion, he managed to free himself, then he and Farah got the children out of the van. Farah received some cuts when she crawled out.

Bradley suffered a fractured right arm and a bad cut on his left forehead that required six stitches.

Daniel suffered numerous cuts on his scalp, his right ear and under his right arm, plus skin burns from the seat belt.

Later, the Frattas received $135,000 compensation from the company who had rented the vehicle involved in the accident to the family. When Lex Baquer was planning a business trip to London, the Frattas asked him to take the large bank draft, which Bob Fratta endorsed, and invest it over there in a joint savings account in the Frattas' names for the benefit of the children.

Ten months had passed since the traffic accident in Maine. The kids were recovered from their injuries and had quit having bad dreams about the accident. But nothing had changed in the parents' relationship—Baquer knew that for sure. He knew it from his daughter's depression, from her continued rundown appearance; he knew that she was believing more than ever that the marriage was not going to work.

Once again Baquer called his son-in-law. "Bob, what in the hell is wrong, anyway?"

Fratta exploded this time: "It's your daughter that wants the divorce. Your daughter, your daughter, can you get that straight? I don't want a divorce. Talk to your daughter and find out what's going on!"

Baquer asked Farah if she wanted a divorce, as Fratta claimed.

"Dad, yes, I want a divorce. I cannot live with this man. I don't want to discuss all the whys, but I simply cannot live with this man. I must get away from him. There is so much you don't know and I cannot talk about with you. But I cannot live with him."

"Honey, you have three kids."

"I've tried, Dad. I've tried and tried and tried. I'm not going to try again."

On March 12, 1992, employing Attorney James Beeler—a corporation attorney who had done civil work for her father related to his business—she filed for a divorce, a fault divorce alleging cruelty. The petition alleged that "the respondent is guilty of cruel treatment toward petitioner of a nature that renders further living together insupportable."

In a brief family court hearing, Farah was granted temporary custody of the three children, with the divorce and permanent custody to be decided in a later trial.

During a phone conversation, Fratta mentioned to Farah that he was staying at his friend's apartment in Missouri City again. Farah said, "Why don't you get an apartment?"

He did take a six-month lease on an apartment. He was a patient, if conniving, man. But when the lease was about to expire, and Farah still would not let him return, he started thinking things were getting a little serious this time.

He phoned her frequently, but she was adamant: This time he was *out*.

Farah was afraid of him. Word had gotten back to Farah and the Baquers that when the divorce papers were served on Fratta at his friend's apartment in Missouri City, he angrily hurled them away and shouted: "She will be dead before she can ever get a divorce!"

Farah had been frightened by her husband even before that threatening statement. Something in his voice made her afraid. She was reluctant to talk to him, period. She knew from past experience that whatever she wanted to do, whatever decision she might make, she would always end up melting under his barrage of words. He had a bullying ability to control her, to dominate her, and she wanted out from under that dominating control.

She had a tape recorder installed on her phone, so whenever he called now, his words would be taped, and she would not have to talk to him and especially not have to listen to him until she could fully and calmly consider what he was saying.

He also had a tape recorder on his phone, so they only communicated through recorded messages.

Knowing it was recorded, he was more careful what he said, too.

SEVEN

Sometimes Farah Fratta could hardly believe it herself. Here she was seriously thinking of a reconciliation with Bob. After all she had been through, after all the mental anguish and carrying around the application for divorce forms for a whole year before she finally had a lawyer file the divorce petition on March 12, 1992.

Now, her resolve to be rid of him was weakening again.

Overriding her eagerness to be out of this marriage was her concern for the happiness of her three children—the most important people in her life—and what their parents going separate ways would do to their young lives. She had known other broken families, seen what happened to children growing up in a single-parent home.

Oh, there were many courageous women—and men, too—who were doing it and doing it well. But Bradley especially, who looked so much like Bob, looked upon his dad as a hero. A policeman who carried a gun and fought the bad guys. Some of Farah's friends nicknamed Bradley little "Paul" because he looked so much like Bob, whom everyone said resembled a young Paul Newman.

Farah was convinced that children needed the love of both a mother and a father.

If there were some way she could live with Bob, she wanted to do it. Some way other than giving in to the horrible sexual perversions he wanted her to do—such revolting things that she could not even talk about them, except with her lawyer and very, very close female friends.

But Farah was at the point of trying again to save her almost ten-year-old marriage.

Drawing the line at Bob's demands for "something more exciting" than normal marital sex, she would do anything else that it took to make their marriage work, for the future of the kids.

Since the first bitter days after Fratta was served with the divorce papers, her husband had simmered down and they had talked about a reconciliation. Bob had a list of things she had to do if they were to get back together. She had her own list, too, but nothing like his list.

Heading Bob's list was, of course, his insistence on her giving him the kind of weird sex that he wanted. No way could she agree to that. Probably that made everything else moot. But Farah had hopes that somehow she could convince him to consult a doctor and get some professional help.

That is, if he was being truthful when he said he loved their children so much.

Another of his requirements for resuming their married life was that Farah undergo breast implant surgery, so that "you will have bigger boobs," as he put it. He called it "a boob job."

She would agree to that, although she was fearful

of the health risks. There had been so many stories lately about the rash of lawsuits filed by women who were suffering bad effects after the surgery.

He had hounded her about this radical surgery almost from the day they were married.

Friends of Farah who heard about Fratta's wish to resculpt his wife's petite and stunning body thought he must be one of those guys who are never satisfied with even the best. One of those nerds who think that "big" is what counts.

At five foot, five inches, weighing 125 pounds, having dark brown hair and brown eyes with some green in them, a beautiful face, a soft voice and a smile that captured everyone's heart, Farah drew lingering looks wherever she went. Plus, she was a highly intelligent and personable woman.

And with all of her good looks, she had an aura of sincere friendliness and kindness. People said that when she entered a room, she brought the place alive, as if a spotlight had picked her out of the crowd.

The breast surgery was performed in August 1992. About a month later, when she was almost healed, Bob Fratta moved back into the house on Forest Fern Drive. They were not together for long. After only two weeks, they separated again.

Farah said only, "He won't change his ways." Fratta had told her that he would not abandon his sexual high jinks. Besides the scatological aberrations, he still wanted an "open marriage" in which both he and Farah could have affairs with other partners, wanted her to take part in three-way sex with him and another man or another woman, and with him and a lesbian or a transvestite or with a lesbian or another man while he watched, or him with another woman while Farah looked on.

He still talked about being "a late bloomer" who had not lost his virginity until age twenty-two, and as a result of that backwardness or timidity or whatever it might have been, he wanted to encourage his kids to have sex at age twelve.

Farah Fratta summed it all up in a deposition given in preparation for the divorce trial and permanent custody case:

"After I filed for divorce early in 1992, my husband and I attempted to reconcile our marriage. As a condition for getting back together, my husband insisted that I have breast surgery.

"Even though I considered the dangers to my personal health, I felt that it was in the best interest of my children that I try to resolve the problems with my husband, and I therefore agreed to the surgery. In August of 1992 the surgery was performed.

"His lifestyle is not conducive to properly raising children. My husband has strange morals. He wanted me to say it was all right if he had sex with other women during our marriage.

"He uses steroids and is more concerned about making his body look good than anything else. This drug use often causes mood swings during which times he becomes aggressive towards the kids.

"Bob does not have any parenting skills. He constantly brings the children home dirty and not fed. Bob has left the children alone without supervision and has gone to the gym to work out.

"Through our marriage Bob has engaged in sexual abuse of me.

"I have been afraid to make this known, and

ashamed to admit that I let him get away with it until now.

"However, because of my daughter, I now believe it is necessary."

Amber then was three-and-one-half years old.

Farah Fratta's hopes of her husband's mental rehabilitation about sex and the restoration of their marriage were forever dashed.

After taking the big gamble to salvage the marriage for the children's happiness, Farah Fratta had now swung 180 degrees, wanting to protect them from what she was certain were existing dangers from their father's presence in the home.

Among those dangers, besides Fratta's abnormal sexual interests, were such behavioral quirks as his keeping a four-foot boa python snake that had bitten Bradley on the back, allowing the children to play with live ammunition, and permitting them to handle and examine his gun. He had left them at times with no proper supervision.

But Farah was especially worried about the safety of her little daughter around a father who was so preoccupied with such depraved sexual deviancies and fantasies.

As the case moved ever so slowly toward its day in court, Fratta also gave a deposition in which he responded to some of the accusations made by his wife, refusing outright to answer some of Beeler's, his wife's attorney, questions.

Steroids: He used them as prescribed by doctors, six weeks at a time, then off for two months. He said he started taking them in 1991 and quit them two months before surgery for a herniated disc.

He had suffered the spinal injury when he stepped in a hole in the lawn at the Missouri City fire station where he was on duty, he said.

Open marriage: He told his wife, after her threats of divorce, why didn't they consider an open marriage in lieu of divorce. He said he had seen shows on TV where those open marriages were successful, kept a marriage going as opposed to divorce. Have your marriage and fun, too, sort of thing.

Had he asked his wife to perform unusual sex acts?: Not those she's talking about, never.

What was meant by "late bloomer?": Well, his ethics and morals were quite high. He had waited until he was twenty-two-years old before he lost his virginity. He called that being a "late bloomer."

Sex for children at twelve: Yes, he had said he thought his children should engage in sex at age twelve, but he was joking about it in relation to his having been a "late bloomer."

Bradley bitten by pet snake: Bradley lay down on the snake and it bit him. So Fratta took this snake back to the pet shop to exchange "for a more docile snake." He said it can be determined whether a snake is a "docile" snake by playing with it. He made the mistake of not being around the first snake enough.

Children playing with live bullets: Being a police officer, he knew that bullets are "completely harmless" unless struck directly with a pointed, pinlike object.

On why he would be the best parent to have the children: A prepared statement he read said, in effect, he was such a good person—a loving, caring, very actively involved father with the children; coached their sports; attended Father Days at school; lectured their classes on safety; was always honest with them;

knows how to commit to his marriage and his children; unlike his wife, always will be there for the children, whether it's personal, scholastic or play; believes he is a better person than his wife and therefore a better example for the children; always would place children's best interest as his priority and teach them to live a good Christian life.

After first agreeing to pay for his wife's breast surgery and charging it to his credit card, Fratta later refused to pay the bill, explaining to the lawyer with a sarcastic remark: "I'm not going to pay for someone else to play with what I paid for."

Farah was alone with the kids again. She was depressed, fearful for her safety, stressed out at work, having little personal esteem. Her doctor prescribed antidepressants. She knew her parents were worried. Her friends were concerned and wondering how to help. She was highly nervous, unable to sleep, growing thinner.

The divorce and custody proceedings were dragging on. Fratta did not have an attorney for the first six months.

Farah's lawyer, James Beeler, spoke with him frequently, by phone and in person at the courthouse in short meetings to discuss various matters regarding the divorce.

Fratta at the start was not opposed to the divorce. He wanted joint custody of the children and property divisions.

The Family Law Code in Texas had changed recently. Joint custody did not mean what it once did—

both parents spending equal time with the children. Under the new laws, one parent generally was given control and primary custody of the children, but the other parent also had all the rights, obligations and duties. The arrangement was known as "joint managing conservatorship."

Although Farah Fratta would have the actual day-to-day care of the three children, her husband as joint managing conservator still would have joint authority and rights in their lives. She told her lawyer she was agreeable to all the divorce settlement terms except Fratta being designated joint managing conservator.

Beeler told Fratta that as long as he and his wife were not in agreement, the law would not give him joint managing conservatorship. Farah would not agree to that because she and her husband lived at distant locations—he in southwest Houston and she in Atascocita. She did not want the children placed under the strain of different and distant locations and neighborhoods.

She wanted to be the managing conservator. She did not object to Fratta having access to their children or to their medical or school records or related matters.

Fratta had never said he wanted sole custody of the children.

Fratta was frank with Beeler in his discussions about the condition of his marriage and what he wanted. (He did not admit any sexual abuse.) As Beeler later testified from the witness stand, "He wanted other women. He wanted other women along with Farah, two women at the same time. He wanted other women outside of Farah, and this, to quote, is the straw that broke the camel's back, and is why she filed. Initially, I don't think he objected to the divorce, but as he went along, he became more belligerent, was basically opposed to the divorce."

EIGHT

Amid the sadness and stress of her disintegrating marriage and the exhausting dreariness of the slogging legal procedures, Farah Fratta was introduced to a young man by one of her close female friends from the airline. His name was David Deitz and he was manager of a local automobile dealership. They met in August 1992.

He was nice looking, friendly and immediately interested in the beautiful Farah Fratta. So pretty and soft spoken and shy, he thought. It had been Deitz's observation that most women as pretty as Farah usually were vain and oversure of themselves and not on the quiet side at all.

Deitz was about thirty years old, and standing six-feet-two and weighing 220 pounds, he looked like the ex-college football player he was. He had played tight end for the Cornhuskers while attending the University of Nebraska, where he graduated with a business degree.

He came to the Humble area in 1990.

Deitz kept in good shape with exercise routines at the President and First Lady gym. There he became acquainted with Farah's friend, who introduced them.

Farah and Deitz both exercised regularly at the

same spa but they had never crossed paths. Usually he was there during his lunch hour, and she worked out in the late afternoon or evening after getting off work.

Farah was glad to learn that Deitz was interested only in the personal health aspects of keeping in shape. He could care less about bodybuilder championships. That pleased Farah. She had had her fill of bodybuilder freaks.

Farah herself was regular in her exercise routine. She was in superb shape. She still went to the gym daily, but managed to avoid Fratta if he happened to be there.

Farah noticed at once that Deitz had a way with youngsters. From the first time he met her children, he liked them. Deitz found them to be lovable kids, sharp and polite. They quickly took to him, too.

Farah and David had lunch together during the week, and their dating mostly was limited to that and going to dinners or concerts or game centers with other couples once a week or so, when the children were staying the night at the home of their grandparents, Lex and Betty Baquer.

The young couple had not started dating until after Farah and Bob Fratta had separated and were getting a divorce.

Oddly, it had been a divorce case plagued with delays for one reason or another—one of them being the death of the judge in whose court the case would have been heard. Farah also would change lawyers two or three times.

On weekends, they did things with the children, going to the local spots where games or other activities for kids were featured—children's game centers, the local McDonald's, the zoo.

Farah, David, Bradley, Daniel and Amber were beginning to feel and act like a family.

There was romance between Farah and Deitz, but they were discreet. As the months passed, they were talking about marriage. In a way, they were unofficially engaged, but everything was on hold until the divorce and custody case was over.

Farah did not want to furnish any legal ammunition for Bob Fratta in their battle for custody of the children.

"The kids were so much fun," Deitz would recall. "They were like my own. I wanted to have a child or two after Farah and I were married, but really those three kids would have been sufficient. I felt that close to them."

Farah kept silent about the sexual abuse that had led to her divorce decision. Farah would never talk to Deitz about the details. "If you only knew—" she said once to him when they were talking about her ravaged domestic life. "But I don't want to tell you, David. I can't tell you."

She said she had never told her parents or brother. It was that degrading in nature. And besides, she was afraid of what Fratta might do. Deitz had heard all kinds of stories from various people who knew Farah well, but he did not push the matter with her because of the emotional stress she felt over the deviant conduct of her husband.

While they awaited the final custody-divorce trial, Fratta did not outwardly aggravate his estranged wife during this time, except in small ways.

He would pay the child support that had been ordered in the earlier temporary custody hearing, but he was always late, paying it at the last possible moment before he would be hauled before a judge.

Even with David Deitz, he was "overly nice" on the infrequent occasions they would run into each other at the gym. He showed no out-in-the-open aggressiveness toward either Farah or Deitz and certainly not the children.

"He had never hit Farah or the kids when they were living together," Deitz said later on. "He was what I call a chicken-shit type. He did everything behind people's backs. In truth, he is an evil, black-hearted and cold-blooded man. He is as creepy a guy as you will ever meet."

As for Farah, Deitz had rarely known anyone who was as "big-hearted and kind and really a very strong person inwardly. She was a good mother and the children always were first in her mind."

Except for a stressful and fearful few weeks after the early morning terrorist assault on her, Farah, in her happy relationship with Deitz, was becoming more like her old self. The change was apparent to Lex and Betty Baquer and to her close friends. Years later, her father said he was glad that Farah had had those months of happiness with David Deitz, having endured so much unhappiness in her tumultuous marriage to Fratta.

But now, even awaiting the long-delayed custody-divorce trial, Farah's old buoyancy was back, the smile was returning.

She talked calmly now with Deitz even about that June 28, 1994 home invasion by the man in black armed with the horrible stun gun.

She told Deitz that she strongly believed Bob Fratta was behind the attack. She confided to Deitz that she thought she might even know the identity of the weird assailant.

"I think I know who it was," she said. "I don't

know or can't think of his name, but I believe I have
seen him and Bob talking together at the gym several
times." The man she was thinking of had a good physique like her husband, she said. At the spa, she knew
him only casually, a passing "hello" type of acquain-
tance.

Although his name eluded her—she wasn't sure
she had ever heard it—the man she described and
had seen talking with Fratta at the gym sounded like
Joe Prystash, another habitué of the President and
First Lady Spa. She recalled that the intruder with
the stun gun was wearing glasses under his ski mask.

And Joe Prystash wore glasses. But she could not
make a positive identification for the investigators.

While staying at her parents' home, where she had
taken refuge after the stun gun assault, Farah Fratta
wrote a letter to her former attorney James Beeler.
Beeler had moved to Victoria, Texas to set up his law
practice.

Although Farah had employed another attorney to
handle her case after Beeler left the Humble area,
she was still in contact with Beeler, paying him for
the work he had done on her civil case.

On July 18, 1994, she wrote Beeler: "So much
more has since developed with this case, and I am
under extreme emotional distress. I was broken into
at five a.m. two weeks ago and was assaulted by a
man wearing a ski mask claiming to want to talk to
me about Bob.

"Two detectives are working on this case and believe Bob is connected to this incident and he is a
prime suspect.

"However, we have very little evidence to go on,

and I await their investigation with great anticipation. I am currently living with my parents for fear of my life and hope this whole matter can come to a close soon."

The letter was written three-and-one-half months before her slaying at the hands of a killer also described by witnesses as "a man in black."

After staying with her parents about two weeks, Farah moved back to her house on Forest Fern.

On the morning of Wednesday, November 9, 1994, Farah called Deitz to tell him the power antennae on her Honda had dropped off. He said he would bring her his car and have hers repaired at the Honda place across the street from him. Farah was working at one of American Airlines' downtown ticket offices, and she was not far from the Nissan dealership.

Later, after Farah's car was ready, Deitz picked it up. Driving to his auto lot, he noticed the air conditioner wasn't blowing cold air. He called Farah again to tell her he would keep the Honda overnight to get the air conditioner repaired, and they could switch cars the next day.

That was why Farah was driving Deitz's 1994 white Nissan Maxima when she parked in her garage that evening and was shot to death.

When Deitz arrived at his home that November 9 evening, he phoned Farah. He got her recorder.

That puzzled him because she should have been there. She had told him earlier that Fratta was taking Bradley to his catechism class at a Catholic church at 7:30 P.M. before bringing the children home. Their father had picked them up at school that afternoon.

Farah always made it a point to be home at 8 P.M.,

the usual time when Fratta returned with the kids after their weekly visitation with him. One time she had been unavoidably five minutes late and she received an angry call from Fratta saying that if she wanted the kids, she could come get them. She did not want to go to his place.

The outcome of that incident was for Fratta not to return the children until he went to work the next morning at 5:30 A.M. Then he dumped them out in front and drove off.

Now, Deitz was wondering why Farah had not answered her phone. He would try again in a few minutes.

When his phone rang, he thought it must be Farah.

It was Zain Baquer, sobbing and telling him that Farah had been shot and was being rushed by helicopter to Hermann Hospital. Deitz sped to the hospital, which was only a five-minute drive from his place. Zain had said that the family would be there as fast as they could.

He was ushered into a small waiting room in the trauma area. As Deitz sat waiting, a doctor entered.

"Well, she was shot two times in the head," the physician said. "Ten minutes ago she lapsed into a coma."

Oh God, maybe there's still hope, Deitz thought.

Then the doctor said, "Five minutes ago she died."

"I'm going to kill him!" Deitz screamed and slammed his fist into the wall. It had to have been Fratta who did it!

Deitz's loud outcry and violent exclamations brought two security officers rushing into the room. After a few minutes he was too stunned with grief to say anything. He sat down on the floor, crying into his hands.

That was the way that Lex and Betty Baquer found him when they came a few minutes later. Deitz was too much in shock to even speak.

Another hospital attendant came in.

Baquer turned to him exclaiming, "I want to see my daughter! Where is she? Please, where is she? Is she alive or dead?"

"I'm sorry, sir. She is dead." The Baquers burst into loud sobs. Deitz was crying and beating his fists against the wall again.

At home later on, Deitz received a call from a homicide detective asking him if he would mind coming to the office to give a short statement. The officer explained it was part of the investigative routine.

When Deitz entered the homicide office on Lockwood, a detective said it would be a few minutes. The detective said to another detective as he walked away, "Keep him away from shithead."

Deitz knew whom the detective meant. Bob Fratta was in an interview room giving his statement.

After giving his brief statement and voluntarily taking a short polygraph test, which the detectives explained was routine in such cases, Deitz left.

On Sunday, the day after Farah Fratta was buried in a private service that Fratta had been barred from attending, the Baquers, accompanied by Deitz, went to Farah's house on Forest Fern to pick up some clothing and other items belonging to the children. The grandparents and brother, Zain, had visited the house on Friday and removed the children's beds and most of their belongings.

Now, as had been the case on Friday, they did not get anything else from the house except the children's toys and smaller things they had not loaded on the first trip.

Deitz was in an upstairs bedroom when he glanced out the window and was startled to see Bob Fratta drive up. Fratta parked a short distance down the block. The sight of the man whom Deitz firmly believed was behind the murder of Farah sent him into a rage.

He dashed down the stairs and ran outside and was running toward Fratta when he was tackled by Lex Baquer. A police officer who had arrived a few minutes earlier also helped to restrain him. Fratta had already called the police to report that the Baquers were "trespassing" on the property.

NINE

When Bob Fratta was cut loose that Thursday afternoon of November 10, 1994, after over fourteen hours of fruitless questioning about his wife's killing, one of the detectives in the homicide office had hurled the suspect's car keys in his direction. The act reflected the disgust and frustration of the homicide unit toward Fratta's noncooperative and smug attitude.

Although Fratta, with his story of being with his kids at church, seemingly had an airtight alibi for his whereabouts when his wife was gunned down in the garage, he still was the primary suspect in the murder. He was not the "man in black" who fired the lethal shots. His alibi, if verified, eliminated the possibility that he was the shooter. But considering what the investigators had heard so far from the victim's family and friends, her estranged husband loomed as the mastermind behind what probably was a contract killing, as far as everyone in homicide was concerned.

Based on the neighbors' eyewitness accounts, there were two other suspects—the black-clad shooter who fled the scene and the driver of the small, silver, one-headlight car that picked him up. That made three people involved in a conspiracy if Fratta had set it up. To the detectives, it smacked of a carefully planned hit job. They also knew they were a long way from proving it.

Toward that goal, the starting place was St. Mary Magdelena Catholic Church on South Houston in Humble, where Fratta said he had taken his children so Bradley could attend his catechism class.

Detective Ronald Roberts talked to two women church members: the catechism class teacher and the woman who supervised the nursery.

The nursery attendant said she remembered Bob Fratta being there on November 9.

"He came in about 6:45 p.m. He was with his three kids. He came in to leave his little girl and boy while the older brother went to his catechism class."

She explained that the nursery was about one-half block from the church and was not structurally connected to the church building.

"How was he acting?" the investigator asked.

"He seemed real tense. I don't know why. He was kind of in a hurry. He didn't know where to leave the kids and things like that."

The nursery keeper remembered Fratta was neatly dressed, since he was going to stay for a meeting of the families of the youngsters in the class. After the kids finished class, there would be a special short service in the church for the children and the adults, she said.

"I told him that the meeting he was going to should be over about eight or eight-thirty."

However, she said Fratta came to pick up the two younger children before 8:30. She thought it was around 8:20.

"I asked him if the meeting was over already, and

he mumbled something I couldn't hear and left with the kids."

The catechism teacher had the same feeling that Fratta was in a hurry and didn't have his mind on the church event. She said Fratta and his wife, Farah, alternated in bringing Bradley to the catechism instructions on Wednesday night. Other times when Fratta came, he was wearing his gym workout clothing and left after leaving the boy, the teacher said. He had never before stayed for church services.

On the evening of November 9, she had noticed he was neatly dressed in blue jeans or slacks and an open-neck shirt and sweater.

"I think it was about ten minutes to seven when he first came into the room," the teacher recalled. "He came in from the outside and had all of the kids with him and seemed a little distracted. He just seemed sort of like, 'Well, let's do this and get this over.' "

He left to take the two younger children to the nursery. When he returned, Fratta had asked, "Now what do we do?"

"I explained to him that he needed to go in the church and they would have a meeting with the parents."

"Then we would be in with the kids about ten minutes after eight, and there would be a short ceremony and everything would be over about eight-thirty.

"When we got in the church, they were having a candle ceremony that night, and he walked up to me and seemed rather agitated that he didn't get a candle. So I gave him my candle and I got one elsewhere."

The detective asked for the names of some of the members who had attended the service. When he contacted several of them, he picked up on something that really roused his interest.

Some of the members remembered seeing Fratta. His pager had gone off several times. He had gone out to return the calls each time and returned. Detective Roberts located a woman who had seen Fratta using the phone in the church office.

Who was paging Fratta during the church service? the detective wondered. Could it have been one of the hit-job conspirators reporting to the boss?

The next move would be to subpoena the telephone records of the church to track the calls that Fratta had made.

In the meantime, an autopsy was performed on Farah Fratta's body at 7:45 A.M. on the day after the slaying. It was done by Dr. Vladimir M. Purangao, the assistant medical examiner of Harris County.

In his report the doctor stated that he found two gunshot wounds to the head, but one of them was a grazing type wound that would not have been fatal. A bandage could have been placed over this wound and the victim could have walked around, the pathologist said. The bullet, or "missile," as the pathologist described it, had entered the left side of her forehead two inches to the left of the middle and four inches below the top of the head, and exited from the left temple area. The slug passed through only skin and muscle and did not enter the skull.

Detectives reading the report realized the less serious wound had been from the first shot fired by the killer that caused the victim to scream and fall to the garage floor.

Since the first wound was a "through and through"

wound, no bullet was recovered. The bullet fragment from this gunshot had already been found in the child's life preserver hanging on the garage wall.

The fatal shot undoubtedly was fired to make sure the woman was dead. The entry point was in the back of the head, one-and-one-half inches to the left of midline and one-and-one-half inches below the top of the head.

The missile entered the skull and perforated the brain, the report said. The slug was recovered in the right temporal lobe. The bullet caused destruction of the brain.

The shooter had pressed the gun barrel against her head to fire the "coup de grâce" shot.

The grazing gunshot wound was described as a "near-contact wound" with the end of the gun barrel within six inches of the skin when the trigger was pulled. This was indicated by soot and powder stipplings found on the skin.

The cold-bloodedness of the execution was confirmed in black and white in the formally worded autopsy report. The pathologist ruled that "she came to her death as a result of [a] contact gunshot wound of the head."

Deputy R. L. Shield, assigned to the identification division, dropped by the medical examiner's office the next day to pick up the bullet removed from Farah Fratta's body. He turned over the ballistic evidence to Deputy Ferrell.

This bullet and the bullet fragment recovered earlier at the crime scene were evidence that could scientifically nail the triggerman if and when the murder weapon was located.

* * *

Bob Fratta, when quizzed briefly at the crime scene, had told Detective Valerio that he phoned Hermann Hospital to ask about his wife because he wanted to take the children to see their mother before she died.

Following up on that volunteered information, the detectives questioned the hospital employee who had received Fratta's phone call.

Christine Rose Raisaman, a thirty-one-year-old X-ray technologist, was on duty that night, working the 2:30 P.M. to 11 P.M. shift. It was a crazy night. Really crazy. Several major traumas had come in about the same time, around 9 P.M.

Nurses and technologists and doctors were running in every direction to treat victims of a motor vehicle accident, an auto-pedestrian accident, an industrial accident and a rash of minor motor vehicle accidents.

And then the lady was brought in by Life Flight.

At that moment Raisaman was standing in the doorway of a major trauma room. She was getting some cassettes to take more X rays, when the stretcher rolled by her and she noticed the pretty young lady with a bandaged head.

She looks so awfully young, the technologist thought. She saw that the patient was wearing a gold necklace. It drew Raisaman's attention because when taking X rays, a tech is always looking for jewelry that might interfere with the picture

She saw that the necklace had the name FARAH spelled out in gold letters.

The telephone in the busy ER room rang. Everybody else was too occupied to answer, so Raisaman picked up the receiver.

"This is Christine, trauma, can I help you?"

A man said that he was calling to inquire about a Life-Flight female patient that had been brought to the hospital.

"There were several females brought in during the last thirty to forty-five minutes," Raisaman said. "I can't be sure who you are talking about, sir."

The caller said he was the husband of Farah Fratta and that she had a gunshot wound to the head.

"Sir, we can't give any information over the phone."

The man's voice rose. "Well, I need to know if she is alive or dead. I have her kids here. Do I need to bring them in to say their good-byes?"

She had never heard such a question put so calmly. "I'm sorry, sir, but I can't legally give any information over the phone." She quickly handed the phone to a passing doctor.

The inquiry had seemed highly unusual. The caller was very blasé, very matter-of-fact, she thought. It seemed strange to hear someone inquiring about their wife in such a businesslike manner, almost as if making the phone call was a big imposition to him. Just a "get on with it, answer my question" tone of voice, no concern, no emotion present.

The more she thought about the conversation, the more it really bothered her. It was hard to believe that a husband would have that attitude after the recent shooting of his wife.

Eventually, after seeing the TV news and reading the papers about the murder of Farah Fratta, the X-ray tech called the general number of the district attorney's office to report the strange call.

* * *

When Detective Bill Valerio had questioned Bob Fratta on the night of the slaying, he asked Fratta if there were any insurance policies in existence in which he was named as beneficiary. The detective was fishing for a possible motive. and insurance money was one of the most common.

Fratta said there were none.

Pursuing the insurance question, Detective Ronald Roberts got in touch with a representative of a clearinghouse for insurance policies. A clearinghouse attempts to catalogue and keep track of existing insurance policies.

Roberts asked if there were any policies on the life of Farah Fratta in which Robert Fratta would be the beneficiary. There had been a $100,000 life-insurance policy issued in 1989 naming Farah's husband as the beneficiary.

But on February 22, 1993, after the Frattas separated and Farah was planning to file for a divorce, one of the first things she had done was to change the policy beneficiary from Bob Fratta to her three children. Under terms of the beneficiary change, the money was to be shared by the children: thirty-three percent each to Bradley and Daniel and thirty-four percent to Amber.

The insurance company later paid the money to the grandparents for the benefit of the children. The Baquers put it in a savings account for the youngsters.

Detectives wondered if Fratta knew that he was no longer the beneficiary on the large policy.

When they contacted the life insurance company and talked to Karry Lennon, a claims processor, they were not all that surprised to learn that Fratta had phoned to find out when he would be paid the $100,000.

Lennon recalled that Fratta's inquiry was made only three days after his wife had been killed.

The claims processor already knew that Farah Fratta had been murdered. The agent who had sold Bob Fratta the insurance policy immediately had faxed newspaper clippings about the murder to her. The file on the policy already had been flagged.

"Any time that murder is involved in any way, whether the beneficiary is involved directly or indirectly, they flag the file," Lennon said. She added that if somebody dies within two years of a life policy being issued, the policy is classified as "contestable."

Lennon told investigators that when Bob Fratta called, "He was very demanding, arrogant, wanting information on the policy, on the beneficiary. He wanted to know . . . when he could expect payment. He was very cold sounding."

It had struck her as an uncommon approach. "Usually, when they call after a relative's death, they are crying."

The claims processor had told Fratta that "Because it was a homicide, it probably was going to be a lengthy process and probably wouldn't be settled for at least a few months—until the file was closed."

He replied sharply that he wasn't a suspect in the murder. She did not have time to tell him that he wasn't the beneficiary named on the policy, either.

"Once he found out that the policy would not be paid off right away, he got very angry and slammed the phone down in my ear."

So Fratta had lied to Detective Valerio about the insurance. He did have a motive after all—not that any of the sheriff's detectives had ever thought any differently. But now they had pinned down at least a partial motive, though they suspected that more than just insurance money was behind the brutal killing of Farah Fratta.

TEN

The Catholic church's phone records subpoenaed by Detective Roberts revealed that one of Bob Fratta's calls from the church phone was to the number of a telephone pager listed in Fratta's address book under "pager," no name given.

The phone company disclosed that the pager number was registered to a Mary Gipp, who lived at an address on Millstone Road in Humble. It was a new name to the investigators on the case. Detectives learned that Gipp shared the apartment with her younger brother. The regular residential phone there was registered in the brother's name.

Phone company records showed that the Mary Gipp of that address also was the owner of a cellular phone. Detectives asked for records of all calls made on that cellular phone.

Consequently, they found that Gipp's cell phone was used in a series of calls the evening of November 9. One call had been to Bob Fratta's home at 6:28 P.M. Five minutes later, another call was placed to Wyatt's Cafeteria. Also called was Farah Fratta's house at 6:36 P.M.

Three calls were made from the cell phone to an outside pay phone at the Davis Food City, a supermarket located a half mile and less than a minute's drive from Farah's house on Forest Fern Drive. The calls were at 6:57 P.M., 7:08 P.M. and 8:04 P.M.

The last call was only one minute before a 911 dispatcher received a panicky call from a woman reporting that she had watched and heard the shooting of her neighbor Farah Fratta on Forest Fern Drive by a man wearing all black. Who had made the calls and where had they originated? Whoever the caller was, he or she was certainly involved in some way with Bob and Farah Fratta, and probably in the slaying of Farah, considering the timing of the calls, Detective Roberts thought.

There was a period between the time Fratta picked up his children at the school and arrived at the church, and another after he left the church to take the kids to their mother's house, during which his activities were unknown.

Unfortunately, the witness who detectives believed would be the most accountable to fill in those details was the oldest of the youngsters, Bradley Fratta. The seven-year-old was a bright child who looked strikingly like his father.

To put him at ease, Bradley was interviewed with his grandparents present. The solemn-faced little boy related that after he and his brother and sister were picked up at school, their dad drove them to his house. Inside, the children played while their father "made some phone calls."

The children also fed their "pets": a four-foot long boa python named Cleopatra, an iguana named Todd, a dog named Niki and a cat named Prissy, which lived at Fratta's house.

Bradley said that when their father finished his calls, they got in his car and went to eat at Wyatt's

Cafeteria, the kids' favorite eating place. Bradley remembered that he had chicken fried steak, mashed potatoes and green beans.

While they were eating, his dad's pager went off. Fratta stood up and said, "I'm going to make a phone call. I'll be back in a minute."

Bradley said that he could see him talking on the "quarter" phone in the cafeteria. After the call, his dad returned to eat dessert with them.

Fratta used the phone a second time on their way out of the cafeteria.

They drove back to their father's house, where Fratta made several phone calls before they headed for the catechism class at church. Bradley was taken to his class; he didn't know where his brother and sister went, and his dad went "to where all the people sit and listen."

Before going to their mother's house after church, they dropped by a Stop and Go convenience store. The youngsters bought a package of bubble gum. Then Fratta stopped at his house again. Getting out, their dad told them to stay in the car while he made another phone call.

Then they headed for their mother's house on Forest Fern.

As they approached, the children grew wide-eyed at the sight of "all the yellow strips around the house, and a lot of policemen, like you see on TV." The children, who started crying, stayed in the car, and later "we went to our friend's house down the street," Bradley said, adding that the boy who lived there was his best friend.

Bradley said their grandparents and uncle and aunt came much later and took them to their grandparents' house.

* * *

Detectives Mark Reynolds and Roger Wedgeworth drove out to Millstone Road to talk to Mary Gipp, the name listed for the pager Fratta had called from the church.

The detectives stopped in front of a two-story, multiple-apartment unit. Gipp's apartment was to the side at the top of a stairway leading to the second floor.

A pretty woman in her late thirties, with brownish hair and a great figure, answered the door. After the detectives identified themselves, she invited them in.

Following some preliminary conversation, one of the detectives asked Gipp if she owned a pager with the number he read to her.

"Yes, I do. My friend lives with his father, and the father doesn't have a phone. I bought the pager and gave it to Joe so I could get in touch with him."

She identified "Joe" as Joe Prystash. She said she had been dating him several months.

"Do you own a cellular phone with this number?" The detective showed her a different number they had found on the phone records for a cellular phone on which several calls had been made to Miss Gipp's pager.

"Yes, that's the number of my cell phone," Gipp said. "What's this all about, anyway?"

"We are investigating the murder of Farah Fratta," one investigator said. "Did you or Joe know her or her husband, Bob Fratta?"

Gipp said she and her friend knew both of them casually through the President and First Lady gym, where all four worked out regularly.

"Where was your cell phone on the afternoon of

November 9?" Reynolds asked. "That was the day she was killed."

"It was in my car. I had used it on the way home. I talked to my boss."

She said she was employed as office manager for an oil and gas company.

"Where did you put the phone when you got home?"

"I just left it in my car."

She said she put it in a small console in her car, which was parked in front of the apartment. She usually left the car unlocked, she said.

"When the car is right in front of the apartment, I seldom lock it."

"Did your friend Joe know where it was?"

She said he did, but as far as she knew Joe never used the phone on that evening.

"Where were you and Joe that evening?" Wedgeworth asked.

She said they were in her apartment, watching a TV program. She named the program.

"Do you have any idea who could have used your cell phone that evening between six P.M. and eight P.M.?" Reynolds asked.

"As far as I know, my phone was in the car where I left it. The next morning it was still where I put it."

The detective asked Gipp if she would give them a statement.

She declined.

One of the detectives mentioned that she probably would be subpoenaed before a grand jury then, where she would be asked to give a statement.

"I'll tell the grand jury the same thing I told you. It's the truth and that's all I know about it," Gipp said.

* * *

Back at the office, the investigators ran a computer check on Gipp and Prystash to see if either had a criminal record.

Nothing was found on Gipp, but Prystash had a rap sheet. He had been involved in a series of burglaries in Dade County, Florida, in 1977 and eventually was placed on probation. He also had been charged with attempted murder in Montgomery County, Texas, in an assault on his brother-in-law, but the charge was later dismissed.

Prystash was unemployed, sometimes working on automobiles, the detectives learned.

They felt that Mary Gipp was not leveling with them about what she knew. They planned to talk to the district attorney's office and determine what their next move would be—probably a grand jury subpoena for Miss Gipp.

The homicide investigators also intended to visit the President and First Lady spa to talk to the bodybuilding crowd to see what they knew about Bob Fratta.

If the life of fictional fantasizer Walter Mitty was secret, the life of sexual fantasizer Bob Fratta was anything but that. It was more like an open book.

Once detectives started exploring the personal address book taken from Fratta's car trunk, they decided that Bob Fratta had been trolling in off-limit romantic waters for several years without the "open marriage" treaty he had sought unsuccessfully with his wife—an agreement wherein they could remain together but have sexual affairs with other partners.

* * *

Detective Valerio scanned the pages of the little book.

There were references to Allie, Debbie, Marian, Natalie, and others.

Beside each of the names and their phone numbers, Fratta had listed data including physical descriptions. With women who had children, even the kids' names were noted.

There was Angela, "a gorgeous blonde, tall, w.o. [works out], goes Almeda, met at Post Oak Ranch."

Amy: "Twenty-one-year-old blonde/blue, PFL [President and First Lady]."

Kerry: "Spinner, used to be blonde, now brunette."

Coretta: "B/F, twenty years old, works Velocity at Sharpstown [Texas] with Bryan."

Jenna: "Beautiful blonde. Goes to Cap B. on Fridays."

Jeannea: "Twenty-nine-year-old, s/a company, PIA's friend."

Kim: "Met Nov. 14 at Colorado, from Las [Vegas], gorgeous brunette."

Kelly: "Call me baby. Bruce Cottage in Dallas. Spoke with Mary [maid] Oct. 26, 9:30 a.m. Said Kelly pretty."

The detectives divided the list.

However, one of Fratta's old girlfriends voluntarily called the sheriff's department homicide unit.

She called after hearing on the news that Farah Fratta had been slain. "I thought this [the call] was the thing to do," she said. Her name was Minnie Lawrence.

* * *

Lawrence was thirty-one years old and a desktop publisher.

She and Robert Alan Fratta were introduced over a telephone dating-service line, a computer-operated dating service where males and females could throw their names and special interests in the electronic mixer and eventually exchange phone numbers and talk. What happened after the talk was up to the individuals.

They met on-line in 1989 and soon were getting out of line.

Lawrence was overweight. She was pretty in the face, but had mounds of flesh piled on her frame.

Minnie didn't really remember if she contacted Fratta or he got in touch with her. In the beginning, they had fairly normal phone conversations.

Fratta told her about himself and his wife and his kids. Pretty soon he had started talking about sex.

He was interested in having "phone sex and that sort of thing."

It was "that sort of thing" where things really got randy between the fat lady and the bodybuilder searching for way, way-out sex.

Explaining Fratta's needs, the overweight woman said, "He knew that I was large and he wanted me to sit on his face. And a lot of times he wanted me to go to the bathroom on him. He wanted me to tie his wife up and have sex with him and with her, and I don't remember everything."

Minnie Lawrence said that what she meant by "wanting her to go to the bathroom on him was to defecate on him."

She had first met Fratta in person in April 1990.

"Almost every time he saw me, he wanted either to see my breasts or to play with my breasts, basically, no matter where it was. I thought he was charming, and he seemed to care about his family, his kids, but he actually seemed very kinky in nature, if you will, sexually."

She said they usually talked every month or two months. She had visited him once on his job as a public safety officer in Missouri City, but had never met his wife or his children or gone to his home.

Minnie recalled there came a time in their relationship when Fratta began to talk about domestic problems. This was in 1993 and early 1994.

He referred to his wife as "the bitch," Lawrence remembered.

It was in October 1994 that Lawrence had a phone conversation with Fratta she would never forget. She said it was about a "week after the big flood in the Atascocita area."

She was concerned about him and called. He said that he had not had any flood damage. She asked him how the divorce was going. Then came the bombshell.

"He asked me if I knew anyone who would kill his wife. I said 'No, are you joking?' "

"Yeah, maybe, maybe not," he replied.

She made a remark about, "I may have known someone a long time ago, but I don't know them now." She thought he was joking.

"He asked me if I knew any black people, and we made a joke out of it. Because I'm from Vidor [Texas] originally, and we laughed about it." Vidor had a reputation of racial troubles between whites and blacks, mostly on the part of the whites.

When he asked her if she knew any black people who would do it, she answered, "You've got to be kidding."

And he said again, "Maybe, maybe not."

When Minnie Lawrence heard the news of the murder, she called the sheriff's office immediately.

ELEVEN

The five people talking in one of Houston's all-night diners were a grab bag. It was a night in October, 1993, in the gay bar, adult bookstore, porno movie house section of the city.

There was Penny Adams, twenty, a pretty blond college girl, saucy, cool, and straight; her girlfriend, Toni, who was cut along the same curvaceous lines and also sexually straight; Todd, a nice-looking homosexual man; and a transvestite in drag named Peaches.

Peaches had introduced Penny to Bob Fratta, who said he was a cop or a fireman, or was it both? Everybody was a hybrid except her and Toni, Penny thought.

But Fratta was definitely a male on the prowl. He quickly let it be known his marriage was crashing on the rocks and he was looking for romantic consolation. Where, Penny wasn't really sure.

The handsome Fratta, a Tarzan type, was flirting with Todd. Me, Jane, not Todd, she wanted to tell the hunk. She wasn't sure who Fratta was more interested in, Todd or her, whether he was a womanizer or a bi or what.

Penny was a tad wild in her college girl kind of way.

She didn't have much time to be very wild. Besides college studies—she was a math major—she worked at a downtown department store.

Although she was confused at the moment about Fratta's rotating interests, she was still liberal minded, a freethinker, everybody to their own thing. Different folks, different strokes.

As she and Fratta talked a few minutes, she noticed that he surveyed her with a healthy male appraisal. He was very good looking, a charming guy, good talker, nice smile, nice dresser, very nice physique. He was a keeper, she decided, though his wife apparently didn't think so, from what he said.

Before they went their various directions, Bob got her phone number and kissed her good-bye. With such a short acquaintanceship, too. He didn't kiss Todd, so that was encouraging.

It was kind of a cool, strange interlude.

Fratta phoned Penny Adams. It was just casual conversation at first, but he started getting sexy, usually when they were talking at night. He talked about what he and his friends had done to girls or what girls they had done. Or what he wanted to do with them, and what he wanted to do with Penny. One time he said he would like to do these things with Penny and the girl he was seeing at the time.

There he was, mused Penny, mixing things up again.

Fratta didn't come on with the rank sex stuff at first, merely asking her to come over and stay the night, sleep with him.

Sometimes he was in a bad mood when he called. She would ask him what was wrong, and he would say it had to do with his wife and their ongoing domestic troubles. He always referred to his wife as a bitch.

Penny was working at a Haunted House around Halloween. She invited Fratta to visit the place. She never invited him again. As she put it, "He kind of weirded me out."

The first night Fratta came to the Haunted House, Adams ran out to see him for a minute. She greeted him cheerfully. "Hi, how are you doing? I've just got a second. Gotta get back and scare the kiddies." She smiled and turned to go.

He reached toward her. "Hey, no. Don't you want to give me a hug and a kiss?"

"No . . . no. . . . Really, I must go. Gotta get back in." And she scampered away.

The second night that Fratta showed up at the Haunted House, Penny Adams had the guys she worked with go tell him she wasn't there.

July 28, 1994, was Penny's twenty-first birthday. She was getting ready for a fun night out with her girlfriends.

They had decided to get a fancy hotel room with a Jacuzzi. Penny had been given a coupon for a free room at the hotel. She and her girlfriends wanted to go there to hang out and get away from home.

Fratta phoned Penny that evening. "What are you doing tonight? Want to do something?"

She told him no, that she and some girlfriends were having an all-girl party to celebrate her birthday. Later she was sorry she had mentioned the hotel's name.

When the girls reached the hotel, they parked and went to check in at the front desk. They were walking back to the car to get their luggage when Fratta suddenly came up behind them. He had not been invited, that was for sure. It looked like he had been waiting in a nearby alley.

He offered to carry their bags to the room. Nothing wrong with that, Adams told herself. In a minute, she quickly changed her attitude. Bob sat in a chair and wouldn't leave.

The girls had brought extra clothing, not knowing for sure what they were going to wear. He nodded toward the luggage and said, "Why don't you all go ahead and change?"

"No, I'm not doing that," Penny said.

Fratta turned toward Trisha, one of Penny's friends. "How about you, hon? Will you change in front of me?" Trisha shook her head.

"Aw, what's the matter, girls? Come on, take off your clothes. How come so bashful?"

The girls started leaving the room. Penny Adams said over her shoulder, "We have things to do, Bob. We'll give you a page later on." Say anything to get rid of this guy. She knew she wasn't going to page him.

Fratta grudgingly left.

"Where'd you ever know that weirdo?" Trisha asked.

Fratta called Adams about a week later and she talked with him. He sounded in a bad mood and was again complaining about his wife, which he did frequently these days, Penny thought.

He said there was no way he could beat his wife

in their custody battle for their children because she had too much financial backing from her father, and he could not compete with that.

Another time Fratta phoned and griped that he wanted to do something that night, but he couldn't because he had to watch his kids who were visiting overnight.

Then, out of the blue, Fratta asked, "Do you know of someone who can kill my wife?"

The stunned Adams said, "What!" Her exclamation reflected the pure shock she felt at his sinister question.

"Okay, hurt her a little bit," Fratta added quickly.

"I've got to go," she said and hung up. She did not know whether to take him seriously or not, but she was not going to even talk about something like that.

Adams called her girlfriend Trisha and then went to spend the night at her house.

Penny had confused feelings about Bob Fratta. She had not known his full name until he posed that frightening question. Then she asked around.

Sometimes he seemed nice and sweet and cool to talk with, and other times he was really weird, perverted and awfully mad at his wife.

A few short months later, after Farah Fratta was killed, Detective Valerio found Penny's name and phone number in Fratta's address book. He phoned her, but she was not home. Her female roommate who answered told the detective she would have Penny call him.

The friend went out and found a newspaper that

carried the murder story and gave it to Penny when she came home.

Penny Adams was filled with regret and guilty feelings. She should have done something, she thought. Should have called the police and told them about Fratta's expressed desire to find someone to kill his wife. Oh, if only she had taken that conversation seriously enough to alert somebody.

Later, when she learned from Detective Valerio that her name was one of many women Bob Fratta had listed in his address book, it made her shiver.

The detective let her read the notation in a small rectangle by her name: "Penny, 20 years old, met at Benny's Diner, weekend. Something, 10-16-93. [That was the correct night.] And another date recorded by Fratta: July 28, 1994." Her birthday, the hotel encounter.

There were three phone numbers noted: Her home number, Trisha's, and Todd's.

Adams later admitted when she was questioned that she had "enjoyed talking to Bob, sometimes over a fairly long period of time."

In the big gymnasium where people were lifting weights and pumping iron and otherwise making themselves grunt, just watching all the physical activity made the detectives wish for a cool drink.

It was beginning to look like a lot of people who exercised at the President and First Lady Spa had heard Bob Fratta talk about hiring a hit man to settle his bitter domestic problems. But it had been a well-kept secret until now—at least as far as the cops were concerned.

On this day and any other day in the spacious gymnasium, business and professional people, executives and lower-level employees, men and women, young and old, were doing their daily grind.

The investigators were impressed by the camaraderie and esprit de corps of the place.

It rose to the surface when questions were asked about Fratta and his oft-repeated inquiry about finding someone to kill his wife.

Many of the spa members had been friends and worked out together for a decade or more, the officers learned.

If you were part of the spa, it was reminiscent of being a resident of a little town where families had known each other through several generations. Like a church with a closely knit membership, this upscale gymnasium and training turf for the bodies beautiful had its own devoted and dedicated congregation.

However, when the questions started, no one held back from telling the sleuths what they knew about Fratta, even with this closeness among the body brotherhood.

The tracking down of persons approached by Bob Fratta in his apparent quest for someone to murder his wife was pushed intensely by the homicide unit after Minnie Lawrence, Fratta's phone-sex girlfriend, had come to the sheriff's office to report he was trying to find a killer to do in his wife.

Lawrence said she "thought it was the thing to do," to tell what she knew about Fratta's desire to have his wife killed, in spite of the embarrassment to herself.

Unfortunately, hardly anyone else who knew about Fratta's efforts to contact a killer was alarmed the way Minnie Lawrence had been. They explained later that they thought Bob was jesting or blowing off steam during the frustration of his domestic legal battles.

Day by day, the detectives encountered a growing number of people who had been asked by Fratta to either kill his wife or put him in touch with someone who would. Several of them were friends who worked out regularly at the gym with both Fratta and Farah.

And the surprising truth was that not one had contacted the police to tell of Fratta's dire quest. All of them said they thought he was merely joking—no way could the guy be serious about something as bad as that. Even if he wasn't joking, he was not going to find anybody who would do such a horrible thing, one man said.

Nor did the spa members who were asked that shocking question by their buddy bodybuilder ever mention to Lex Baquer that his son-in-law was trying to find someone to bump off Farah.

Bob Fratta was, in a sense, an admired hero and a leader among his muscle-building peers. They envied him and wanted to be like him—the men anyway.

The ladies just admired his body, period.

Lex Baquer, a congenial spa workout regular himself, who knew many of the members at least casually, was baffled that there had not been any hint of a warning to him or the authorities from those Fratta had contacted. It was something the heartbroken father would never understand.

"They had all known it for weeks, and they saw me there frequently and not a single one ever came up to me and said, 'Hey, Lex, do you know Bob Fratta is asking everybody around here where he can find a hit man to kill Farah?' I will never know why somebody did not say something to me about it."

TWELVE

By now, the detectives were thinking that Bob Fratta must have told half the people in town about wanting to have his wife killed.

The stories they turned up among the gymnasium bodybuilders were beginning to sound like a stuck record on a broken jukebox, playing over and over again.

There was Richard Lee Orlando, thirty-nine, an accountant. He had known Fratta about fourteen years and described him as "a fairly close friend through the gymnasium." He was also acquainted with Farah who he said was "amicable."

Fratta had discussed with Orlando the tough time he was having after he and his wife separated. In the beginning, the accountant recalled, Fratta had not talked about violence toward his estranged wife.

"I think as time went on, the discussion became a little more aggressive in that region. He commented that he wouldn't care if harm were to come to Farah. For instance, one statement was that he wouldn't care if she was 'hit by a MAC truck,' I believe, was the wording."

Orlando remembered another eyebrow raising remark. "If I had a gun, I would shoot her in the head," said Fratta.

For the most part, Orlando said, he thought these were just comments made in the heat of battle during endless legal proceedings.

"Kind of blowing off steam, no big deal, that's how I perceived it."

It had not really alarmed him, Orlando told the officers.

One time, Fratta asked his friend, "You don't know any hit men, do you?"

"No, I do not," Orlando had said with some anger.

"Some Italian you are," Fratta said, jokingly, of course, as the witness recalled.

Fratta's theme was getting a little tiresome. Orlando estimated that his workout partner "made comments about hit men five or six times" a few weeks before the slaying.

"If I had taken them seriously, I would have notified the authorities," he said.

Orlando had phoned Fratta's house early on the morning of Wednesday, November 9, to ask if he would be at the gym that night. Bob said something about having to keep his kids that evening.

Orlando's recollection of their conversation on the day that Farah Fratta would be murdered was that it was a normal exchange during which Fratta sounded like his usual self.

The next morning, Orlando tried to call Fratta at home, but received no answer. It was about 4 P.M. before Fratta finally answered.

Orlando remembered their conversation.

"How are you doing, Bob?" he began.

"I'm very tired."

"What's wrong?"

"I've been up all night."

"For goodness sakes, why?"

Fratta sounded surprised at the question.

"You mean you haven't heard? You don't know?"

"No, I do not."

"You mean you haven't watched the news or listened to the radio?"

"No, I've been at work all day. I haven't heard anything."

"Well, it's been a nightmare. Farah is dead. She was shot in the head."

The news hit Orlando like a punch. But even then, he noticed no trace of sadness in Fratta's words, no trace of concern. He spoke in a matter-of-fact tone and manner, no differently than if he were discussing the weather. It struck Orlando as highly odd, to say the least.

"Guess who the primary suspect is?" Fratta asked.

"Who?" Orlando was too dumfounded to say anything else.

"Yours truly," Fratta said. Again in that flat and ordinary tone of voice.

John A. Ruiz, thirty-three, assistant manager of a large supermarket in Humble, had been working out at the President and First Lady gym for several months. He and Bob Fratta often were workout partners. They talked while doing their routines.

Fratta talked mostly about the troubles he was having with his estranged wife and their divorce-custody case, Ruiz related to the investigators.

Three months before Farah Fratta was slain, Ruiz and Bob Fratta were talking in the gym's upstairs weight room.

Fratta said his wife was taking him for all the money he made and he was getting tired of it. He referred to the child-support payments he was required to make.

"I would be better off if she was dead," Fratta told Ruiz.

Ruiz was mulling that remark when Fratta asked, "Do you know somebody who would knock her off?"

Ruiz was shocked. "Why are you asking me this, Bob?"

"Because you're a Mexican, John. I thought you might know some of your people who would do something like that."

The assistant store manager was upset by the shocking question and the racial bias implied in Fratta's words of "some of your people who would do something like that."

Obviously angry, Ruiz turned and walked away from Fratta and never talked to him much after that.

Ruiz felt that Fratta had sounded serious when he spoke about "someone to knock off my wife."

"I didn't really know what to think, but I didn't think he would do something like that," Ruiz said. "I didn't really talk to him much after that."

James Ray Thomas, twenty-nine, had known Bob Fratta for ten years. At first they were workout partners, but they became close friends. In fact, Bob had been one of the groomsmen in Thomas's wedding.

"Did he discuss his marital problems with you?" a detective asked.

"Yeah," Thomas said. Like the time, after an argument with his wife at her house, Fratta came to the gym in a particularly foul mood. He said something to the effect of wanting to take a 9-mm pistol and "put some slugs in her head," as Thomas recalled.

"I took it as a joke," he said.

The detectives were hearing that frequently. They were starting to think that everybody around the gym must have a great sense of humor.

Thomas remembered another episode. He was driving Fratta to pick up his new Volkswagen when Fratta started talking about how "he needed to get someone to take care of Farah and about the price and different things, how much money it would take."

Fratta had pondered his chances of getting away with killing his wife. He told Thomas he had made a study during his law-enforcement training, and had personally "seen this happen before—several times in fact—and the people got off. Most of them that happened they went unsolved."

It seemed to Thomas that about all his friend wanted to talk about anymore was how he could kill his wife. Fratta said he had been saving up money from extra jobs he worked and now had about $3,000.

Thomas turned and looked directly at Fratta. "Let me give you some advice, Bob, as a friend who cares. You need to go see a doctor, you really do."

He didn't take the advice.

When Fratta kept harping about getting his wife killed, Thomas snapped, "Let's don't talk about it anymore, okay? I don't want to know."

During questioning by detectives, Thomas said, "I asked him one time why would he want to go around and tell everybody if he wanted to do something like that, is he trying to get himself in trouble or what?"

Fratta's explanation was that he hoped to confuse the police, cause more red tape in the subsequent investigation by making more people suspects or witnesses.

All that remark told Thomas was that Fratta still seemed obsessed with the thought of murdering his wife. Thomas still did not believe his workout pal would do something that stupid. My gosh, he was a cop himself, wasn't he?

But Thomas admitted he was anxious enough over the violent remarks that he told his wife some of the things Fratta had been saying.

He added that he had the feeling something bad was going to happen to Farah.

Mike Edens knew his work-out partner Bob Fratta was distraught over domestic troubles. Fratta had gone so far as to mention he wanted to do away with his wife, Farah. Edens was horrified.

For a few weeks he had been trying to help Fratta, get him to go to church with him. He was hoping that Fratta would change his lifestyle. God was the only answer to any problem in our lives, the religious Edens stressed to his gymnasium friend.

"It's going to be okay, Bob," Edens told him. "God will help you with this."

"I've been praying to God, and God hasn't been listening to me," Fratta said.

"You have to give it time, Bob."

Apparently Bob believed he did not have as much time as God might need. For a while he had listened to Edens, and Edens thought he was winning him over. Once Fratta had followed him inside Edens's church and stayed for the service, but that was the only time he ever attended church, as far as Edens knew.

"He didn't want to go back to church with me, and he didn't attempt that anymore, I don't think," Edens told detectives.

"One of the things that Bob was concerned about from the religious standpoint . . . was his understanding of the Bible that divorce was not permitted, people were supposed to remain married," Edens recalled. Fratta never mentioned the Bible's doctrine on murder.

Nevertheless, Edens admired Fratta's great physique and how he had achieved it with his workout techniques. He felt guilty about being so envious. He often talked with Fratta about it, wondering if he himself could ever get such wonderful results. Edens sought his advice frequently about bodybuilding.

He was trying a special protein drink Fratta had recommended, but he could not tell if it was helping or not.

Edens told the investigators he was devastated when he heard about the murder of Farah Fratta. He went to the funeral, arriving as they were closing the casket.

Bob Fratta came by Edens's apartment after the funeral to talk.

He asked Edens if he would like to go by the house where Farah was slain. Edens declined.

Later that evening, Edens and Fratta happened to meet accidentally at a restaurant. After the meal, Fratta gave him a ride home, and he came inside to talk again.

Edens was surprised at his friend's composure. He didn't seem sad over his wife's death.

After a short visit, Fratta got up and said, "Well, I guess I'll go."

Edens called after him, "Hey, stay out of trouble."

Fratta stuck his head back through the door and said sarcastically, "What could be worse than capital murder?"

The detectives then interviewed Fratta's fellow officers in the Missouri City Public Safety Department. Missouri City was only a short distance from Houston. The Harris County Sheriff's detectives figured they would get some candid information.

"Generally, Bob is a friendly guy, and he's intelligent, but he works on his own agenda most of the time," said Officer Mike Melton. "I mean the things that go on operate around Bob's schedule, what Bob wants to do—besides emergency calls, of course.

"I thought he was rather perverted," the officer said. "I guess his biggest fantasy that he tells everybody about was wanting to have a woman shit on him."

Melton said Fratta was depressed and angry about the divorce his wife had filed, "particularly about problems he was having with his wife's dad." Melton recalled a conversation he and Fratta had while taking showers at the fire station during a shift change. "I was getting off duty and he was just coming on duty.

"He was saying that he couldn't afford the child support payments. It was taking all of his money, and besides, her dad was supporting her, that sort of stuff."

Melton said they were talking about ex-wives. Melton was divorced and ironically his ex-wife lived only two blocks from Farah Fratta.

"It will get better in time, Bob," Melton said.

But Fratta said it wouldn't.

"He commented to me that we could both solve our problems if I would kill his wife and he would kill mine," Melton recalled. "He said he wasn't going to pay her. He would kill her and be out in five years and get his kids back, but he wasn't going to pay her. He was that adamant about not paying the child support."

Melton said he thought Fratta meant what he said. "But he also was blowing off a lot."

Melton told the investigators that when he heard Farah Fratta had been murdered, "I thought that he did it."

Jerry Parker, a former shift partner of Fratta's, described him as "vain and set on himself."

"He talked about his sexual preferences, such as being with more than one woman and having other men present. He liked to show off with his women. To my recollection, he liked to have women defecate on him."

One day while they were the only ones in the fire station, Fratta had been making numerous phone calls and seemed despondent, Parker recalled.

"He was upset about the child custody matters and he said, 'I'll just kill her and I'll do my time, and when I get out I'll have my kids.' I told him it couldn't be that bad, we've all been there, you know. Just take it easy, cheer up!"

THIRTEEN

That terrible night of November 9, 1994, when Farah Fratta was shot to death in her garage, Lex and Betty Baquer pledged they would immediately seek custody of their three grandchildren.

Two days after the slaying, the day before the funeral, Baquer employed a new attorney to file a completely new lawsuit seeking the custody of the children for their grandparents, plus child support from Fratta.

The hearing on Farah Fratta's divorce-custody suit had been scheduled for November 28, 1994, but now with filing of the new lawsuit by the Baquers, everything had to start over.

With the mother's death, Bob Fratta, as the surviving parent, naturally would be in line to get custody of Bradley, Daniel and Amber.

The Baquers were dead set that was not going to happen.

From the start, their daughter's divorce and custody case filed by her on March 12, 1992, had been delayed countless times. Now, the same thing was happening. The family court judge in whose court the new case was filed, had been gravely ill for almost a year and had recently died.

Family Court Judge Robert Hinojosa had won the death-vacated family court bench after a hard-fought election.

Barely having taken office, the judge realized he was inundated by scores of cases that had piled up during the absence of the ailing judge, even though substitute judges had sat in his place.

Judge Hinojosa started work immediately to give preferential setting to needful cases. He worked late hours as he strived to line up seatings for the backlog of cases.

In the interim between the murder of Farah Fratta and the setting down for trial of the Baquers' lawsuit, another judge had made a ruling enjoining Bob Fratta from seeing the children.

The father's attorney was raging at the door of the newly elected Hinojosa, bitterly complaining that his client had been denied access to his children for these many weeks, unable to seek legal relief from the temporary order.

Fratta was seeking to get the children from the grandparents, with whom they had been since their mother's slaying.

At a brief hearing on December 2, 1994, the Baquers' attorney told Judge Hinojosa that there was evidence that linked the killing of Farah Fratta to the children's father.

Fratta's attorney sharply denied the accusations, and told the judge that the children themselves said Fratta has been a good father who never harmed or threatened them.

"Police officials say if Fratta proves his innocence, they will back off," said Fratta's lawyer. "But that's not according to the laws governing our country. He shouldn't have to prove his innocence. This so-called 'investigation' could go on for years, and the damage will continue to be done to the children.

"Your Honor, he has every right to his children."

But the Baquers' attorney told the judge that she believed that, regardless of the outcome of the police investigation, there was evidence to implicate the father in the killing.

Hinojosa delayed the case until December 14, 1994, saying he hoped the sheriff department's investigation into the murder would be concluded.

"I know that whichever way I go in this case, I am in error. But I would rather err on the side of the children." Hinojosa conceded that he "might be committing a serious injustice" to the father, but he was keeping the children with the grandparents "out of an abundance of caution" until the conclusion of the criminal investigation when he could make a final decision.

Unlike a criminal court in which guilt must be proven "beyond a reasonable doubt," a judge's or a jury's finding in a civil court is based on "the preponderance" of the evidence instead of "beyond a reasonable doubt."

When the December 14 hearing of the case began, the sheriff's office investigation was by no means finished.

The testimony was as lurid as expected and also unusual in that Farah's lawyer, striving to prove Bob Fratta was an unfit father who should be denied custody, would introduce evidence to show that he was involved in the murder of the children's mother.

That was something hardworking detectives of the sheriff's department also wanted to prove and were working around the clock to get it done. But the probe was stalled, although Bob Fratta was the primary suspect and had been from the first day of the probe.

They were still a long way from taking their suspicions before a grand jury to seek an indictment.

Although they had plenty of witnesses who could testify that Fratta had tenaciously solicited several people to kill his wife or to recommend someone who might, they had no idea at this point who the black-clad trigger man and his accomplice in the one-headlight getaway car might be.

On the opening day of the hearing, five witnesses testified that Fratta had asked if they or someone they knew would take money to kill his estranged wife. The witnesses said they thought Fratta was only kidding or joking around, a story that was a familiar one to the ears of the homicide investigators.

John Ruiz, the supermarket assistant manager, again related that Fratta had approached him while they worked out.

"He said he would be better off if his wife was dead. He asked me if I would kill her, or if I knew anyone else who would knock her off."

The manager of a tanning salon, Jason Terry, testified that Fratta asked him about committing the murder for $3,000.

"He felt because he was a police officer, I don't have to worry about anything," said Terry. "He said we could set it up and handle it so nobody would get caught." The salon manager said he refused the offer and never saw Fratta again.

Another bodybuilder friend, James Ray Thomas, employed as a roofer, described how he was approached by Fratta about killing his wife for money.

Thomas also thought Fratta was joking around as usual.

"We just always joke a lot together at the gym, so I took what he said jokingly. We were always laughing and cutting up."

Witnesses testified that Fratta's alleged motive for killing his wife was to end the two-year-old custody battle originally begun by his wife and to put an end to child support payments.

Homicide detectives believed the father not only wanted to end the support payments, he wanted to get access to the $100,000 insurance policy on his wife's life, a policy he thought still bore his name as beneficiary. The homicide detectives believed that he also wanted the $135,000 that was in a savings account in England designated for the benefit of the children.

One witness was Penny Adams, the college girl whom Fratta had tried to hit on for sex, not murder-for-hire.

"Her parents were rich, and they kept putting money in to make the case go forward," Adams testified. "He didn't think that he had the finances to stay with it any longer and win."

She also testified that Fratta was on a first-name basis with transvestite prostitutes that she knew. She said Fratta tried to get her into a sexual encounter with him and another man.

There was testimony about Fratta's bizarre, perverted sexual practices that drove his wife to seek a divorce and the sole custody of their children. Repulsive and sickening acts such as asking her to defecate in his mouth, urinate on his face, beat, kick and strangle him while he masturbated, and engage in three-way sexual acts with him, another man or another woman, or both. He wanted to watch her have sex with a lesbian or a transvestite, according to testimony.

There were also stories by witnesses that Fratta wanted an "open marriage" in which he, and Farah if she so desired, could have sexual trysts with other partners and remain married for the sake of their children.

In another vein that Baquers' lawyer said showed Fratta to be an unfit father, witnesses told how he allowed the children to play with live bullets. His response to that accusation was: "It's no different than any other little toy."

Other dangers to the children, as related by witnesses, was the "pet" boa python that had bitten his oldest boy, Bradley, on the back as the boy played with it. Fratta's story was that Bradley had lain down on the snake.

Fratta said after the python bit his son, he took the snake back to the pet shop and exchanged it "for a more docile python."

Fratta's attorney called him as a witness. Not many minutes had passed before Fratta invoked the Fifth Amendment on grounds his answer might incriminate him.

He did not claim the fifth to one question from his lawyer. He readily affirmed that the children wanted to be with him and said, "I am a loving father."

Only when the Baquers' attorney tried to question him about the murder of his estranged wife did Fratta invoke the fifth over and over.

His lawyer objected vigorously to this line of questioning, arguing that the hearing was not a criminal proceeding and that the allegations concerning his part in the homicide had no bearing on his fitness as a father.

The objection was overruled.

Lex Baquer testified that he and his wife had shielded the children from publicity; the children only used the TV to play video games or to watch video movies, he said.

The grandfather testified that he had done nothing to turn the children away from their father.

"We've just said that their daddy is helping catch the bad guys. We've left it at that. They burn candles and pray for their mother every night," Baquer said.

The courtroom was silent and tense on December 15 when Judge Hinojosa announced his ruling. He awarded custody of the children to the grandparents.

The judge declared that he believed from the evidence that Fratta had been involved in the murder of the children's mother. Judge Hinojosa blasted Bob Fratta's character when he announced his decision.

"I cannot imagine a more grievous harm to the children than for their father to induce the death of their mother, who was raising them," said the judge. "Your conduct and judgment are seriously impaired."

Looking sternly at Fratta, the judge said, "As for nurturing love and care, I don't think you understand what that means."

The judge explained that none of the testimony about Fratta's lurid sexual encounters had led to his ruling. The father's implication in the slaying of the children's mother was far and beyond enough reason.

But Judge Hinojosa did say that "in twenty-three years of family-oriented legal work," he had "never heard this degree of depravity . . . and bizarre sexual behavior."

After the judge announced his ruling, the courtroom audience burst into a display of tears and cheers. Many of the spectators were wearing yellow ribbons in support of the grandparents.

Lex and Betty Baquer wept and hugged each other.

Baquer told the news media: "It was a good decision. We will do our very best to raise them as they should be raised—as good honorable citizens of the U.S. They are in good hands."

With tears running down her cheeks Betty Baquer said of her former son-in-law, "He's a monster. It was so very hard hearing how my daughter had to suffer and endure her pain from this man."

At the request of the Baquers' attorney and a court-appointed lawyer representing the children, Judge Hinojosa ordered Fratta to pay $488 a month in child support to the Baquers. The father was also ordered to maintain health insurance for the children.

The judge said that mental evaluation tests of the children, ordered by the court as part of a psychological evaluation of both the parents and the children, showed that the children remained fond of their father—although they had been shielded from news of the criminal investigation against Fratta.

He said that the shielding was to continue, along with his ban of any comment to them about the alleged complicity of their father in their mother's death.

The existing supervised visitation of Fratta with the children on every other Saturday was continued in the judge's order. Fratta also was allowed daily fifteen-minute phone conversations with them.

The ruling had no impact on Fratta in regards to

the ongoing investigation of him as the main suspect in his wife's murder. He had not been charged in the murder of Farah Fratta.

After the judge read his ruling, Fratta left the courtroom quickly and declined to make any comment to reporters.

Shortly after Judge Hinojosa's ruling in the custody case, the City of Missouri City fired Fratta from his job as public safety officer.

Fratta had been suspended with pay since November 15, following his questioning by sheriff's detectives as the prime suspect in the slaying of his wife.

Missouri City Fire Chief Danny Jan, in announcing the dismissal of Fratta, said city officials "determined it was no longer appropriate for Mr. Fratta to continue working as a public safety officer with the city at this time."

Bob Fratta had $488 a month in child support to pay at this time and no job.

FOURTEEN

Lex Baquer went back to work at his auto paint and bodywork business a few days before Christmas 1994. He was on his way to talk to a customer when his pager went off. He saw that it was his office number; he returned the page on his cellular phone.

The office manager answered. His voice sounded different. He said, "Sir, there has been a problem. This guy came in making a commotion. There are police all over the place. The guy said something to Ann like someone would make an attempt on your life."

He said that Ann, the office secretary, had fainted.

Baquer pulled his car into the parking lot of a store and dialed the Houston Police Department, giving his location and telling the dispatcher he needed protection. Within a few minutes a Houston patrolman pulled up.

Lex told the policeman what happened at his office. The officer said, "How do you know it wasn't some irate customer?"

"Look, just stay with me a few minutes," Baquer said. Then he phoned the sheriff's office and got Detective Ronald Roberts and repeated details of the call from his office.

"Stay put where you are. I'll be there," the detective said. Detectives Roberts and Harry Fikaris arrived within a short time.

Roberts told the city police officer, "We'll take care of it. We know what it's all about."

The sheriff's detectives escorted Baquer to his office. Detectives had heard reports that Fratta had told people that he was trying to get custody of the children because "if someone had killed their mother, they might do something like that to her parents as well." Whether it was a veiled threat was not known, but it was not inconceivable to the investigators that Baquer could be targeted.

When the badly frightened secretary was able to talk, she related what had happened.

She said she was doing some filing in another room when she heard the office door chimes go off. She looked into the office and saw a tall man wearing dark glasses, a leather jacket and leather gloves and dark trousers.

She said to him, "Yes, what can I do for you?"

"Where's Lex?" the man asked gruffly.

"He's not here right now," the secretary said. She was growing apprehensive because of the visitor's actions and appearance.

"You're a damn liar!" the man exclaimed.

"Excuse me?" the startled secretary said. And then she repeated, "He's not here. He's gone to see a customer."

The man strode quickly across the room and kicked open the door of Baquer's office. He saw it was empty.

On the way out, he grabbed a flowerpot and hurled it back through a window.

"Tell Lex I'll be back!" the man shouted.

The secretary saw him drive off in a car with dark tinted windows.

Then she had fainted.

Could the strange episode be related to the murder case? the detectives wondered. They decided they couldn't take chances.

Roberts drove Baquer to his house and told him and his wife to pack their bags. "I think we need to get you away for a day or two, just to be on the safe side."

He drove them and their grandchildren to a farm about seventy miles away. He and other detectives remained with them for the next few days.

The day before Christmas, Baquer told Detective Roberts, "I've got to get back. There are things I must do."

They returned home, but detectives were assigned to watch the house. During the time under guard, the children started calling Detective William Valerio "Uncle Bill."

There were no further threats or incidents. The mystery of the violent office visitor never was cleared up.

The phone rang and Lex Baquer answered.

"Is this Lex Baquer?" a man's voice asked.

"Yes?"

"I know who killed your daughter." Baquer's heart started beating faster.

"Who are you?" Baquer asked.

"I'm somebody," the man said.

"Unless you are going to give me a name, I am not interested in talking to you."

"For the time being my name is Bill." The caller said he was a police officer.

"You've caught me at the wrong time. Can I call you back somewhere?"

"I'll give you a pager number."

After he hung up, Baquer phoned Detective Roberts and told him what had happened. Roberts instructed him to wait until detectives could tap his phone to listen to the conversation and record it. After this was done, Baquer called the pager number given to him.

Baquer said he was interested. "Bill" said he was a police officer out of the Dallas area. He named a restaurant where they could meet and talk.

"I'll be wearing a baseball cap. I'll recognize you. I know who you are. But you don't know me."

The detectives made preparations to monitor the conversation. They gave Baquer a cellular phone that was bugged.

"Just put it on the table when you go in," said Roberts. "He probably knows you carry a cell phone. If he wants to make any calls, tell him he can use your phone."

Several detectives would have the meeting place under surveillance, inside and out. They wanted to be ready on the chance it was a plot to harm Baquer. The officers scanned the restaurant area carefully ahead of time. The detectives, scattered inside the restaurant, had electronic equipment to monitor the conversation.

Baquer admitted he was nervous.

A detective said, "When you get out of your car,

walk fast and in a zig-zag pattern. You won't be an easy target if someone is trying to shoot you."

The detectives would move in at any sign of an ambush.

When Baquer entered the restaurant, a large man wearing a baseball cap rose and gestured to him.

"I'm Bill," he said. "You want something to eat?"

Baquer said he wasn't hungry, and then told the man, "I don't know you. I want you to put your hands on the table and keep them there. How do I know you aren't going to kill *me?*"

The man laughed and placed his hands on the table.

The would-be hit man told Baquer that he worked for a large syndicate of lawyers who used police officers to do these jobs. He said he was a mercenary who liked his job.

"Do you know my son-in-law?" Baquer asked.

"I know the name, read it in the paper. I don't know him personally."

They talked for about an hour, then set up another meeting. They left separately.

Later, Baquer got in touch again through the pager number. They met at a pizza place in Humble. Baquer was under the same surveillance by detectives, both inside and outside the eatery.

This time "Bill" got right down to business. He would kill Bob Fratta for $10,000. He said Baquer would never hear from him again after he did the killing.

"I don't have that kind of money," Baquer said.

"That's all right. I trust you, Lex. You can pay me when you get it."

The man said he would kill Fratta with preconcealed dynamite, would do it this very night.

"Okay, if that's what you want to do," Baquer said.

They shook hands. Baquer went to his car and drove home.

The listening detectives had all they needed.

They closed in and arrested the man as he sat in his Jeep. They found a 9-mm gun, a rifle and explosives in his possession.

The suspect was identified as William Edward Planter, forty-seven years old, of Hoffman, Texas. Detectives learned he was a former deputy sheriff in a Texas county and a former police chief of a small Texas town. He was confined in the Harris County jail on a charge of trying to arrange the murder of Robert Fratta. His bond was set at $20,000.

Detectives said Planter envisioned himself as a "Rambo type" of mercenary. He was a big reader of soldier-of-fortune type magazines.

After the arrest hit the news media, one of Fratta's lawyers voiced concern that Fratta had not been alerted that he might be a hit target. Said the lawyer, "If this was an effort to solicit someone to kill Bob Fratta, why didn't they say, 'Hey, Bob, there's someone out there trying to kill you?' "

Thinking of the numerous people Fratta had solicited to kill his wife, none who ever notified the authorities, the homicide detectives couldn't help but see the irony.

Planter later was tried in district court and received a prison sentence of nineteen years.

Meanwhile, the murder of Farah Fratta remained unsolved, but the homicide investigators were about to bear down on two people they believed knew what had happened.

FIFTEEN

Mary Gipp had to be the key to breaking the case, in the thinking of Sergeant Dan Billingsley and his squad of detectives. The phone records had pointed to her as the owner of both the pager and the cellular phone used in the series of phone calls believed to be related to the murder.

Gipp claimed she had bought the pager to give to Joe Prystash because he was living with his father at New Caney, and his father did not have a phone. She and Prystash had been dating and sleeping together for several months. She paid for the pager because Prystash was not working; that was why the pager was in her name, although it was in the hands of Prystash.

In recent weeks, Prystash had been staying, off and on, in Gipp's apartment, she said. Her younger brother also lived there.

Mary Gipp said that she and Prystash were watching an ice-skating show on TV at the apartment during the critical time period on November 9.

Mary reiterated that she left the cell phone in her car when she got home from work on that Wednesday, and it was still there the next morning.

* * *

The detectives had had a piece of luck. All the calls made from the Catholic church where Fratta was before and after his wife was slain were on record. Usually local phone calls are not a matter of record with most phone companies, Sergeant Billingsley knew.

It happened that the phone company serving the church with a measured local service was one that had records of local calls.

During the last part of November, Sergeant Billingsley and Detectives Roberts and Valerio all talked to Mary Gipp. One time, Roberts was joined by his wife, Sherry, who was a deputy in the criminal warrants section. The investigators thought the presence of another woman might help in dealing with the sometimes volatile Gipp.

Once when detectives were at the apartment, Prystash happened to come by. He agreed to go down to the homicide office voluntarily for questioning and a polygraph test.

When questioned, he did not deny that Fratta might have called his pager on the evening Farah Fratta was killed. But he was sure he had not returned any calls from Fratta on that date. He said he frequently did not return calls to his pager from Fratta because "I don't like the guy."

Prystash was given three separate tests by polygraph examiner David Rainey.

The tests indicated that Prystash was being deceptive when he answered five questions: Who shot Farah Fratta? Were you there when she was shot? Did you shoot her? Did you talk to Bob Fratta on November 9? Did you know she was shot before you saw it on TV?

Billingsley had mixed feelings about the accuracy

of polygraph tests. Much depended on the background and character of the test subject. He had seen suspects flunk a test who had nothing to do with the case they were questioned about and nothing to hide.

Sometimes a subject with a background of trouble with the law might show up as lying on a test simply because he had done so much illegal stuff in his life that he registered as lying.

In the sergeant's opinion, Prystash could easily be in that category. He was an ex-con with a record of burglary and other offenses in several states. In a burglary of a department store in Dade County, Florida, Prystash, carrying a long-blade knife in his waistband, had fought furiously with the patrol cop who caught him inside. The officer had to bang the burglar's head on the floor to subdue him.

He was cool, but he was mean as hell, from what the detectives could learn. Standing about five feet eight, with a bodybuilder's physique, a narrow, angular, pockmarked face (probably from steroid use), Prystash was hard to read, even by experienced interviewers.

He was soft-spoken, showed no outward reaction to anything and had cold-looking eyes.

Later, while going over notes of the various interviews with Gipp and Prystash, Billingsley and the other detectives agreed to focus on Mary Gipp. If they could provide the leverage, Gipp probably would spill everything.

There had been no peace of mind for Mary Gipp for a very long time. Now time was running out again.

She had been in a state of numbness and shame

and fear for all these weeks that stretched on so slowly, ticking away like the timing device on a bomb.

Now, she again was up against an unresolvable dilemma like the one she had faced during the weeks before the murder of Farah Fratta, when she could have saved her life.

She knew she had to do something this time—it was her own life involved. If she did not take action, she was sure she was going to jail or even prison. The detectives were closing in.

Not only that, if her boyfriend ever found out what she had done after the murder, she was in real danger of losing her life.

It had been this way before Farah's slaying. Gipp had intended to warn her early in the week that it had happened.

She had been unable to concentrate at work on Monday, November 7, so she left the office early to get her address book and call the potential murder victim. But she could not find it. She was not sure she would have called Farah, even if she had found her phone number.

Then came that fear-paralyzing time when she knew it was too late to do anything.

She knew exactly when it would happen. She could have saved Farah's life. Mary's heart pounded and she was sick to her stomach, but she could not pick up the phone and call the police.

Hardly a day had passed that the sheriff's detectives did not question and re-question her—about the pager, about the cell phone, about Joe Prystash for whom she had an intense love that she could not rationalize.

Life with Joe was like living in a bad dream, where

you are running and running to get away, but being pulled back even closer to the nightmare you are trying to escape.

And yet, there was a thrill in living on the edge of danger, in the shadow of disaster that loomed so close in her life with Joe. She knew he had a criminal background, had spent time in jail and prison, was a hard and unemotional man whose cold eyes were penetrating.

Yet, he spoke in a soft voice and loved her in a way that belied his ruthlessness and his strange, calculating inner self.

But, oh, how she loved the guy! God help her, she loved him so much and would do anything—anything—to retain his love, that was as threatening as an untreated cancer.

She was not a *bad* woman. She was intelligent, held a good job, worked hard, liked people. In her late thirties, she was striking in appearance.

She first met Joe Prystash in January 1993, at the President and First Lady gym. He worked out regularly, and so did she, almost daily, for two or three hours. He did not have a steady job, but he was taking classes at the Universal Technical Institute to become a mechanic.

Sometimes he made a little money working on the cars of people he knew. She helped him financially. She had paid for the damn pager so she would have a way to keep in touch with him.

She knew Bob and Farah casually, through the gym, but she had been unable to think of their last name back when she wanted to make the warning call.

Now, once more, time was running out—this time for her.

She recalled that evening when she and Joe were watching the TV news, the day after the murder, when Bob Fratta held his press conference in the parking lot at the sheriff's department after he was questioned at length.

She remembered how he smiled and even laughed and smirked when he talked to the reporters. Joe had said then that if Bob didn't stop grinning and laughing on TV like that he was going to be in bad trouble.

And so was she, Gipp had thought, if Joe learned what she had done when he came home that awful night following the murder. If Joe found out, she knew she would be dead.

Besides that constant fear of Joe finding out, she was facing another serious crisis now. The persistent homicide detectives were certain she was withholding vital information about the murder of Farah Fratta and said if she continued with her noncooperative conduct, she could be charged with murder.

When she declined to make a statement, the detectives said she would be subpoenaed before a grand jury. If she did not cooperate with the grand jury, she could go to jail herself.

That is, if Joe did not kill her first, she thought.

It was high noon in Gipp's precarious life.

As February 1995 came to an end, the inevitable happened. Gipp was at work when she was served with the dreaded subpoena to appear before a Harris County grand jury.

The ticking bomb was about to go off.

She and her lawyer met with Assistant District Attorney Dan Rizzo on March 1, 1995, and went before District Judge Mary Bacon. At this time, as prearranged in a conference between Gipp's attorney and the assistant D.A., Gipp was offered immunity from prosecution on a charge of tampering with evidence if she would testify truthfully before the grand jury and later, if and when it came to be, at a murder trial or trials.

After this agreement was approved by the judge, Gipp went before the grand jury to tell her story. Having been given immunity, Gipp could not invoke the Fifth Amendment when quizzed before the investigative body.

On Friday, Gipp met with Detective Roberts. They were in Assistant District Attorney Rizzo's office. Rizzo and Gipp's lawyer were present. Her lawyer turned over to the detective a Ziploc bag containing a small piece of blue paper that Gipp said bore the name and serial number of the gun that Joe Prystash had unloaded in Gipp's apartment after the murder.

She told Roberts what she knew about the murder and agreed to make a formal signed statement the next day.

Gipp and her lawyer came to the homicide office on Saturday, March 4. She said to Roberts, "The guy that shot her already is in jail. He is one of those guys that robbed the bank the other day."

She said his name was Howard Guidry.

That afternoon in Detective Roberts's office, Mary Gipp gave and signed a statement about the nightmarish events of Wednesday, November 9, 1994, that had haunted her for over four months. The memories still were all too vivid in her mind.

She was unable to concentrate at work, and had left for home about 4:30 P.M. on that fateful Wednesday. She had known for more than a week that the murder of Farah Fratta was set for this date. When she arrived at her apartment, she encountered Howard Guidry, a young black man who lived with relatives in the apartment directly across the landing from hers.

He was sitting on the landing at the top of the stairs. She saw that he was dressed in a black knit shirt and black jeans.

Gipp said hello and asked Guidry, "Where's Joe?"

"I'm waiting for him," Guidry replied.

Gipp went into her apartment. A few minutes later, Joe Prystash came in the door. She saw that he was wearing a black cotton shirt with a black hood attached, and black jeans.

When he entered, Gipp was talking to a female friend on the phone. She waved and continued her conversation.

Prystash left about two minutes later in his four-door, silver Nissan, a small compact car that had one nonworking headlight as the result of an earlier accident.

She knew that Guidry had left with him.

She knew that they were on their way to kill Farah Fratta.

A few minutes later, Gipp was still talking on the phone when she received another call. She had call waiting, so she put her friend on hold and answered.

It was Prystash. He said he was checking to see if the cell phone was working. It was the phone Gipp had purchased for him.

Prystash and Guidry returned to the apartment unit about 8:30 P.M. Guidry went into his apartment.

Gipp was watching television when Joe came back. He didn't say anything, but walked back to the bedroom, and she followed him. She saw that he was unloading a gun, and he went and tossed two shells into the garbage can in the kitchen. The gun apparently had been concealed under his shirt when he came in because she had not noticed it.

Gipp asked her boyfriend, "Did you kill her?"

"Yes," he said. He added that Guidry had killed her in her garage.

After throwing away the two bullets, Prystash returned to the bedroom and hid the gun under some clothing. He said he had to meet Bob Fratta at the gym and left.

It had happened. Gipp felt sick and faint. That the two men had killed Farah and she had known they were going to do it for weeks and had not done anything to prevent it began to sink in.

She went to the kitchen and took the two shells from the garbage and dropped them in a Ziploc bag and put that in her filing cabinet. Then she entered the bedroom and removed a brown-leather gun case from beneath a pile of Joe's clothing on a shelf. Inside the plush sheepskin-lined case was the revolver.

She picked up a small blue notepad and wrote down the identifying information visible on the gun: "Police Bulldog .38 Special Charter Arms Corp., Stratford, Conn., 77150." And the serial number: "77191590."

She returned the gun to the case and slipped it back under the clothing. She put the blue slip with the gun information in another Ziploc bag and then into her filing cabinet with the two shells.

The next morning, Prystash told her what had happened the night before. He related that Howard Guidry, after being dropped off at Farah Fratta's house, was waiting for her in the garage and shot her once in the head, and then she fell back and he shot her again. Guidry called him at a pay phone where Prystash was waiting as planned and said he had done it and was ready to be picked up by Prystash.

He used Gipp's cellular phone that Prystash had given him, along with the .38-caliber police special that Fratta had given to Prystash to pass along to the shooter.

Prystash picked up Guidry and they returned to their apartments.

The next morning, November 10, Prystash came back with a newly purchased headlight and replaced the headlight that was not working. They had heard on the news the night before that witnesses had seen a car with only one headlight pick up the man in black after the shooting.

Eventually Prystash had the car crushed at a salvage yard.

He also gave the gun to Guidry and told him to get rid of it, throw it in the San Jacinto River, Gipp recalled when giving her statement.

Therein lay a big complication. Prystash had gone that night to the President and First Lady spa to meet Fratta, who was to give him the $1,000 in cash promised to Guidry for the hit job.

Of course, Fratta was not there. He was being questioned at the sheriff department's homicide office.

Guidry was upset after finding out Prystash could not get his payoff money since that money was in the glove compartment of Fratta's car where it was found by Detective Valerio.

When Prystash gave him the gun to get rid of,

Guidry kept it. At least he had something to show for his work.

A week or two later, after detectives had come to talk to her and searched her house but found nothing, Gipp had put the shells in the soil of a thick potted plant in the apartment.

On another day, when she and Joe were going shopping at a mall, she thought of the slugs and did not want to leave them in the apartment. She put them in her pocket.

At the mall, she reached in her pocket for money and felt the shells. She had forgotten she was carrying them around. She panicked and hurried to a nearby trash bin where she dumped them. Joe was in a store at the time.

SIXTEEN

Early on Monday, March 6, Detective Roberts went to the robbery division of the sheriff's department. There he talked with Detectives William "Bill" Moore and Tommy Keen, the two investigators who had worked the armed robbery of the Klein State Bank in the Humble area on March 1.

From the two robbery detectives, Roberts got copies of their reports on the incident.

The Wednesday the Klein State Bank had been hit by three masked men ironically was the same day that Mary Gipp had started talking and bargaining with the grand jury and the district attorney's office.

On two fronts events began unwinding that would break the Fratta murder investigation wide open.

The bank was not busy at about 12:30 P.M.

Paulette Sanchez Scott, the teller supervisor, was occupied with routine duties when she glanced toward the front door and saw three black men rushing inside and pulling down ski masks over their faces. One man wore a red ski mask that had openings only for his eyes and mouth, and the other two were in similar white ski masks.

They all had guns in their hands.

"Oh, my God!" she exclaimed and was reaching under the counter to set off the robbery alarm when the first of the masked men through the door suddenly was in front of her, brandishing a big gun and yelling, "Back up, bitch!"

He kept the gun leveled at her until a second gunman made a one-handed leap over the counter. Chantel Pave was bending over in the teller spot next to Scott, intent on pushing her alarm button when the robber shoved his gun in her face and also commanded, "Back up, bitch!"

The third bandit, wearing the red ski mask, sprinted into the bank's human resources area and aimed his gun at Gene Hoverdale, vice president in charge of that department. He would always remember that this day happened to be his wedding anniversary. Fleetingly, he wondered if he would live to see another one.

Paulette Scott could see a red dot dancing across Hoverdale's white shirt. The gunman shouted at Hoverdale, "What are you doing, mother fucker? Get down and don't look at me!" Then he asked threateningly, "Did you all set the alarm off? Did you hit the alarm?" He was waving the gun back and forth. The red dot that the bank official recognized as a laser gun sight was dancing around on his white shirt.

"No, there is no alarm in this office," Hoverdale said quickly, trying to speak calmly and hoping to settle down the hyped-up bank robber.

Hoverdale then got down on the floor. The robber in the red mask with the laser dot gun sight yelled, "Turn your head and don't look at me!"

The vice president was on the floor behind his desk, his head turned to the right. He saw the red dot circling around his head and he thought he was going to be shot any second.

One of the gunmen grabbed teller Pave by the elbow and pulled her toward him with his gun pressed to her head. The man who had burst through the door first rushed to the teller on duty toward the back of the bank, Susan Blair.

He put one hand on the counter and nimbly vaulted over to confront Blair with his weapon, yelling the now-all-too-familiar phrases of "Back up, bitch!!" and "Fuck you, bitch!" as he loomed over her.

Scott believed she was going to be killed. One of the gunmen wearing a white mask had his arm extended over the two-foot-wide counter, his gun aimed directly at her face.

While the one bandit kept the women covered and spit out a steady stream of obscenities at them, the thug in the red mask targeted Hoverdale under his laser-sight gun. He was shouting, "All of you get down on the floor!"

Scott recalled later that she must have been in shock and did not respond fast enough to suit the man in the red mask. He turned toward her abruptly and snarled, "Do you think it's funny, bitch?"

His quiet deadliness caused her reflexes to kick in gear. She quickly answered, "No," and dropped to the floor, expecting the impact of a bullet from the laser-sight gun any second.

The man who had jumped the counter began grabbing the money from the cash drawers and jamming it into a green backpack the robbers had brought with them.

Suddenly the bandit in the red mask, who was walking rapidly around the main customer area, shouted "Let's go! Let's go! Let's get out! Let's go!"

He seemed to be the leader, giving all the orders as he covered the bank employees with his vicious-looking, laser-sight gun.

The robber who had been stuffing the backpack with stacks of money one-handed it back over the counter. They dashed out the door. Only minutes had passed, but the blitzlike robbery had seemed like an eternity to the terrified tellers and bank vice president.

Tellers Scott and Pave crawled over to their alarm buttons and set them off. Scott grabbed a phone and called the police. She gave descriptions of the robber trio to the dispatcher.

A customer ran up to the front door just as one of the employees shouted, "Lock the door!" The tellers wanted to make sure the gunmen did not come back.

A short time earlier, Connie Peterson, who worked at a travel agency, had made a deposit in the bank, and then she and her husband, Bob, parked their car at the nearby Burger King to eat lunch.

When they emerged from the hamburger place about 12:35 P.M., Connie Peterson was startled to see three masked men with guns in their hands dash out the bank door. She couldn't believe what she was seeing. For some reason the thought flashed through her mind and she passed it along to her husband: "That's just like in the movies! It looks like they just robbed the bank!"

The couple watched the armed gang jump into a gray Ford Escort parked in the Burger King parking lot. Another man was sitting behind the wheel. The wheel man burned rubber as he swung the car around and sped into the street.

"We've got to do something!" Bob Peterson yelled. "Come on, let's follow them and see if we can get a license number!"

At the moment his wife was thinking more about going the other way.

"Bob, do you think we should do that?" Connie murmured.

Obviously he did. Their car gained on the fleeing robbers.

"Don't get too close, please!" his wife cried.

They stayed behind the getaway car only long enough to see there was no license plate on it. But they obtained a good description of the vehicle.

Peterson turned around and returned to the bank. It was him beating on the front door which had been locked in his face. He saw that a man inside the bank was talking on the phone, he guessed probably to the police. Peterson caught the attention of the man and shouted a detailed description of the bandits' car— make, model, color and the fact that there was no license plate on it.

Deputies Frank Javie Gomez and J. E. Freeman of the traffic division were on their motorcycles and working stationary radar in the 400 block of West Richey on this early Wednesday afternoon.

It was 12:40 P.M. when their radios crackled with an "all officers" bulletin from the dispatcher. A robbery had just happened at the Klein State Bank on Kuykendahl. The bank was about three miles away from the motorcycle officers' location.

The dispatcher reported that three black males had fled the bank in a gray Ford Escort, headed south.

The traffic deputies remained on their radar assignment, pending further word on the bank robbery.

Ten minutes later, Gomez clocked a vehicle speeding at fifty miles per hour in the thirty MPH zone on West Richey. He locked in his radar. When the driver apparently noticed the uniform officers, he slowed down rapidly and made a quick turn into the driveway of a private residence.

Gomez told his partner, "Joe, that looks like a Ford Escort over there. That's what the bank robbers are supposed to be driving." Gomez knew his partner owned a Ford Escort himself and he should know.

"It's a Ford Escort all right, and there are three or four black guys in it," Freeman said.

As the officers watched, a black man got out of the car and walked up to the house where they had stopped in the drive. The officers were about one hundred feet away, but it looked as if the man was knocking at the front door.

The deputies observed him return to the car and open the trunk and remove something. To get a closer look, the officers rode their motorcycles over to where the vehicle was parked and stopped on the shoulder of the road.

The man was putting a license plate on the back of the car.

At that point Gomez advised his dispatcher that they might need backup because it looked like they had spotted the bank robbery car and suspects—a gray Ford Escort, no license tag, with three or four black males in it—one of whom was now attaching a license plate.

The man who had been putting on the license called to Deputy Freeman: "Why you all harassing

Last photo ever taken of Farah Fratta, 33.
(Photo courtesy Lex S. Baquer)

Robert and Farah Fratta were married on May 7, 1983.
(Photo courtesy Lex S. Baquer)

Beautiful Farah Fratta was a devoted wife and mother for nine years before her husband's bizarre sexual requests caused her to sue for divorce. (*Photo courtesy Lex S. Baquer*)

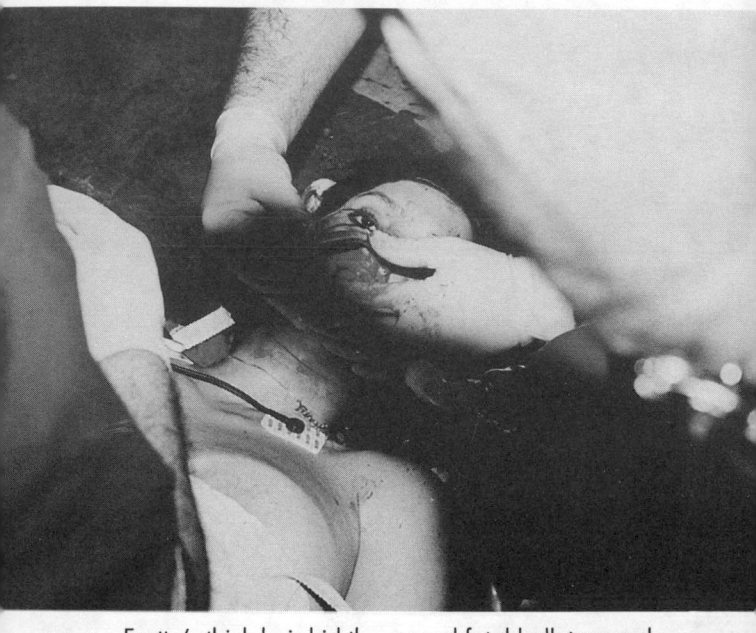

Fratta's thick hair hid the second fatal bullet wound.
(*Photo courtesy Harris County, Texas Sheriff's Department*)

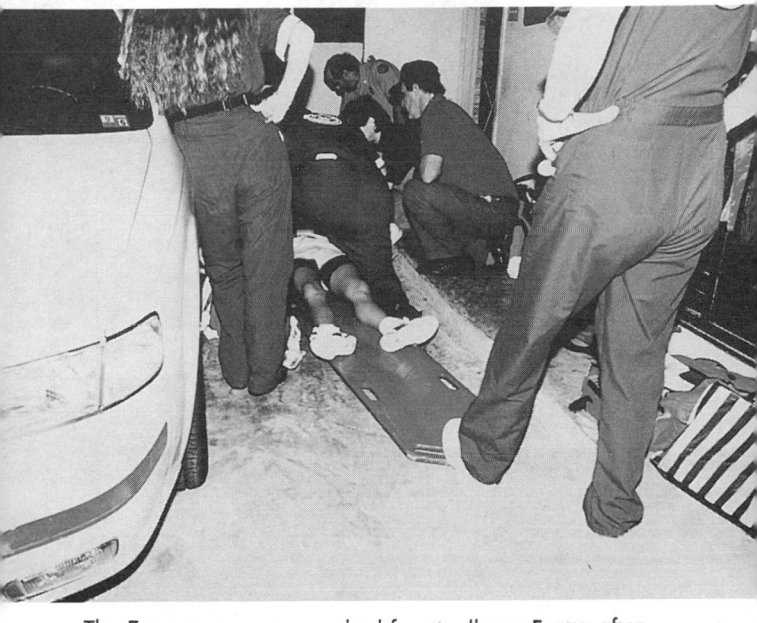
The Emergency crew worked frantically on Fratta after responding to the 911 call from her neighbors. (*Photo courtesy Harris County, Texas Sheriff's Department*)

Fratta's workout shoes and socks were removed by
the Emergency crew.
(*Photo courtesy Harris County, Texas Sheriff's Department*)

Police were later able to match with the murder weapon fragments of the two bullets found while searching the Fratta garage. *(Photo courtesy Harris County, Texas Sheriff's Department)*

Blood covered the garage floor after Fratta was taken to the hospital by helicopter.
(Photo courtesy Harris County, Texas Sheriff's Department)

When arrested for armed robbery,
Howard Paul Guidry was carrying the gun
he used to kill Farah Fratta. (*Photo
courtesy Texas Department of Corrections*)

Joseph Prystash asked Guidry to help him
kill a friend's wife. (*Photo courtesy Texas
Department of Corrections*)

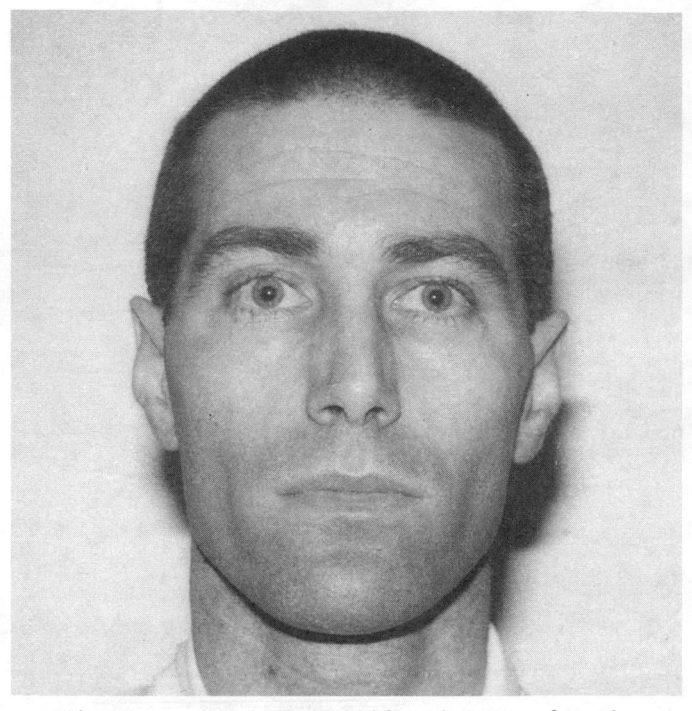

Robert Fratta, 39, was arrested for solicitation of murder.
Charged with capital murder, he received the death penalty.
(Photo courtesy Texas Department of Corrections)

Detective Ronnie Roberts.
(*Photo courtesy Ronnie Roberts*)

Lieutenant John Denholm
(*Photo courtesy John Denholm*)

Lex and Betty Baquer, Farah's parents.
(*Photo courtesy Lex S. Baquer*)

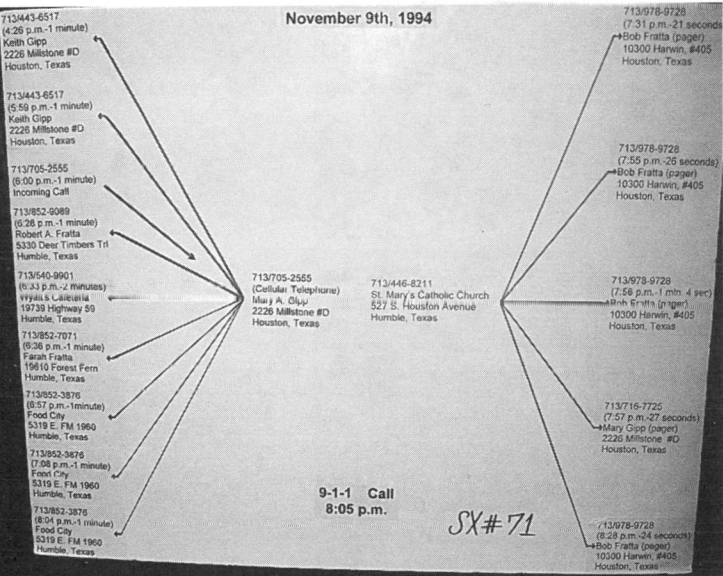

Phone calls made between Robert Fratta and Joseph Prystash on the night of the murder showed Fratta was behind his wife's murder. *(Photo courtesy Lex S. Baquer)*

Lead prosecutor Kelly Jalufka Siegler (*Photo courtesy Kelly Jalufka Siegler*)

Co-prosecutor Casey O'Brien (*author's collection*)

Sheriff's Department homicide unit and victim's family. (*Left to right*) Capt. Candy Henderson, Det. Harry Fikaris, Sgt. Danny Billingsley, Lex Baquer, Det. Jim Hoffman, Donna Baquer, Det. Bill Valerio, Betty Baquer, Zain Baquer, Det. Greg Pinkins, Det. Ron Roberts, Det. Larry Davis and Det. Mark Reynolds. (*Photo courtesy Lex S. Baquer*)

Farah's gravesite with floral tribute from her children.
(Photo courtesy Lex S. Baquer)

me? I'm visiting my auntie." That was the wrong thing to say.

Both officers had worked traffic in this neighborhood several times in the recent past, and they knew that a white family lived at that address.

The other three men started to get out of the car. Gomez ordered them to get back inside. All four piled back into the Ford. The car was started suddenly and backed toward the officers on their bikes.

Gomez and Freeman drew their guns and ordered the driver to stop. Seeing the drawn guns, the driver swerved through a nearby ditch and took off at high speed.

Gomez radioed the dispatcher that the two officers were in pursuit of the bank robbery suspects. It was a high-speed chase, with sirens going and red lights flashing.

The fleeing car roared west on Richey to Ella, then north on Ella to North Forest, where it turned east. Spotting a police car that already was in the area, the driver made a quick right.

The car roared north on Summer Wind for about half a block, then braked to a near stop and the occupants bailed out, with the car still moving slowly.

Two men exited from the right doors and ran through the yards of some residences, and the other two took off to the east. Gomez ran in pursuit of the pair running east and his partner ran in the other direction after the others.

One of the suspects that Gomez chased was carrying a green backpack. He and the other man darted between some houses and jumped a fence. By the time Gomez reached the fence, the two fugitives already were going over a second fence.

They headed toward a wooded area.

As Gomez ran as fast as he could and hurtled the first fence, he was beginning to lose his wind. Several motorists honked and pointed toward Ella Street and the nearby woods.

Gomez, breathing hard, returned to his cycle and drove around to Ella. He was northbound on Ella when he spotted the man, still carrying the bag, standing near an automotive center.

They stared at each other. Gomez was on his bike. He shouted for the suspect to raise his hands. But the man turned and ran through the woods and on through a group of houses.

Gomez jumped from his cycle and renewed the foot chase. He was thinking he didn't have much chance of overtaking his speedy quarry. He noticed that money in bank wrappers was tumbling from the backpack.

Gomez was trying to catch the runner before he got over a fence again. He managed to grab a leg, but the man struggled free of his grasp.

Gomez jumped the fence. The deputy was gaining on the robber, who suddenly stopped and threw up his hands and yelled, "I give up! I was just driving! I didn't do anything else!"

"Get on the ground," Gomez ordered. The suspect stretched out and Gomez handcuffed the man's hands behind his back.

The deputy radioed his dispatcher that one suspect was in custody. A patrol car arrived within minutes and took charge of the cuffed prisoner.

Gomez then walked to where the backpack lay on the ground about fifteen feet from where the man surrendered. Gomez signaled to another officer to secure the money that fell out on the other side of the fence.

Gomez learned from radio traffic that the other three robbery suspects had been caught.

Detective William Moore of the robbery division arrived to coordinate the search and take charge of the scene. Moore's partner, Detective Tom Keen, worked the scene at the bank.

Examining the green backpack, Moore found three guns, two white and one red ski mask, and slightly over $12,000 cash still in bank wrappers. Also in the bag was a pair of "sapping" gloves—black leather gloves with sand on the knuckles. The sandy knuckles caused painful, serious damage to anyone struck with the gloves, the detective knew. These guys meant business.

The weapons removed from the backpack included what Moore referred to as a Mac 11 or Mac 12 with a laser sight, a short-barrel revolver loaded with six rounds of ammunition, and a longer barrel .38-caliber Police Bulldog Special Charter Arms revolver with no rounds in it.

After talking to Detectives Moore and Keen and reading over the reports, Roberts next went to the property room where all evidence is kept in storage. There he signed out for the .38 Police Bulldog Special Charter Arms revolver.

He looked at the blue slip of paper on which Mary Gipp had written the serial number of the gun reportedly used to kill Farah Fratta, the gun Joe Prystash had unloaded and concealed in her apartment.

The serial number matched the one on the gun from the bank robbery.

The murder weapon had been found and along with it the suspect named by Mary Gipp as the shooter.

Howard Guidry was one of the four bank robbery suspects arrested. His photograph later was picked out of an array of photos by teller Paulette Scott. She definitely identified him as the bank robber who wore the red ski mask and had the gun with the red-dot laser sight. Scott said, judging by his actions, she thought he was the leader of the gang.

Detective Roberts's next move was to contact the Alcohol, Tobacco and Firearms Bureau, a federal agency that keeps track of all registered guns in the United States.

He asked the ATF to run a priority check to learn the identity of the original purchaser of the gun.

The report that came back showed that the buyer was Robert Alan Fratta. The purchase form was signed by him. He had used his Texas driver's license as identification. The gun was bought from Carter's Country, a gun distributor on Treschwig in the northeast part of Harris County. It was purchased on October 31, 1982. Fratta had signed his name at the bottom of the purchase form.

SEVENTEEN

Detective Ronnie Roberts also read Guidry's confession to the Klein bank robbery that he had made to the robbery division detectives. The statement spoke worlds about the eighteen-year-old.

He was born in Louisiana on April 15, 1976. Guidry had been involved in petty law-breaking in his boyhood, but his first run-in with the cops of any degree of seriousness happened in Lafayette, Louisiana when he was sixteen.

A patrol cop spotted the teenager prowling the parking lot of a movie theater in north Lafayette at 10:10 P.M. on a Saturday. There were plenty of cars to prowl on Saturday night. The policeman discovered that several on the lot had been burglarized. Guidry was arrested and charged with five counts of simple burglary of a vehicle, but as he was a juvenile, he got off with a light tap on the wrist.

The youth moved from Louisiana to the Houston area in August, 1994, and lived with his sister in the apartment on Millstone. He got a job at a supermarket on Highway 1960, close to where he lived, but the job didn't work out.

Mostly he was footloose and needing money when he first met Joe Prystash, who lived in the apartment across the landing. Guidry thought Prystash was a cool dude, a bodybuilding type who had been around, even pulled some time.

They both liked to sit on the landing and smoke. That was how they met. Smoking and talking, talking about money.

Money was Guidry's driving force. He was into some drugs in a minor way when he could afford it, but had no big habit.

Talking about money was how Guidry fell into the worst deal of his young life. And it was a need for money that got him busted on the bank robbery rap.

Roberts read Guidry's robbery confession. The statement was given after his arrest on the day of the heist at 6:45 P.M.

Guidry related he went to the apartment of his friend, Brian, about 9:30 A.M. Two other guys were there: Andre and Stinky. He later learned Stinky's real name was Shawn.

"We were all talking about how we would do anything to get some money," Guidry said.

Guidry had said to his buddies, "Maybe we ought to go rob a McDonald's. Somebody said, 'No, we ought to rob a bank.' "

They left about 11:30 A.M. in the gray Ford Escort that belonged to a relative. He drove.

Along Highway 1960 they spotted a Bank United, but decided there were too many people and traffic was too heavy.

Guidry was turning around in a Burger King parking lot when they noticed the Klein State Bank nearby. Not much business, noontime lull maybe. Little traffic.

Guidry, Stinky and Andre would go in. Brian would do the driving. Guidry reached under the car seat and withdrew his Mac 12-1-380 with the laser sight. He stuck it in his waist band.

Guidry had a red ski mask. The other two wore white masks. They put them on and rushed through the door, yanking their masks down over their faces, showing guns, yelling for everybody to get down.

Andre jumped over the counter and laid down money on it from the cash drawers. Guidry started stuffing the money in the green backpack they had for that purpose.

After they sped from the bank, they drove only a few blocks when Brian spotted two motorcycle cops.

Guidry then described the chase that ended in their capture.

On the morning of March 7, the day after Detective Roberts had conferred with the robbery division detectives, he laid out the case against Guidry to Sergeant Billingsley and his colleagues. The next step was to grill Guidry on the Farah Fratta murder.

Everybody agreed the best man for that job was Detective James Hoffman, a six-foot-one, 280-pound, broad-shouldered, sandy-haired detective with a reputation among his fellow detectives as one of the top interrogators in the business. Sergeant Billingsley speaks of Hoffman as "a damn good murder cop."

Later in the afternoon, Roberts phoned the off-duty Hoffman at home and asked for his help.

They drove to the downtown Harris County Jail to pick up Guidry and brought him to the homicide office on Lockwood.

As they guided the handcuffed suspect to their car,

Hoffman sized him up. He was about five-feet, ten-inches tall, weighed around 180, had a noticeably round face and short hair. He kept silent on the ride to the homicide office.

The detectives put him in Interview Room 1 and let him wait while Roberts filled Hoffman in on what he knew about the suspect and the bank robbery that Guidry readily had "upped" after his capture.

Hoffman preferred to work alone when questioning a suspect. He was friendly and made small talk with Guidry. He did not read him the legal rights card immediately. He would do that soon enough, certainly before any questioning started, but first he wanted to relate to the suspect and put him at ease.

Guidry was not talkative at all. He eyed the big detective and answered questions with a word or two. They talked about Guidry's family in Louisiana and he said he missed them.

Finally, Hoffman read the blue card of legal rights to Guidry, and asked if he wanted an attorney present. Guidry said no. Then Hoffman began reciting what they had learned about the murder of Farah Fratta.

He said the investigators had definite information from solid witnesses who had put the finger on Guidry and Joe Prystash. Hoffman intentionally downplayed Guidry's involvement at the beginning of their conversation.

It took a time of relaxed and unhurried talk to convince the suspect they had enough to tie him to the homicide. Taking his time, Hoffman wanted to establish a rapport with the young man, let him know that he was not a push-and-shove type of cop. But he wanted the truth about how it went down.

He emphasized that the investigators already knew how the killing happened, based on their knowledge of telephone calls that had been made from the murder scene and other locations, plus having definitely identified the murder weapon through ballistic comparisons of test-fired bullets and the slug found in the life preserver on the garage wall.

He added that detectives also had interviewed unnamed witnesses who had indisputable knowledge of the murder conspiracy and those involved in it.

Eventually, Guidry agreed to make a statement.

Hoffman brought in his laptop computer and Guidry started slowly, with occasional verbal prompting by Hoffman.

Guidry began giving his statement at 11:28 P.M.

So far the suspect and detective had talked for over two hours. It would be a long night.

Guidry related in his confession:

"I first met Joe Prystash around the middle of October 1994. Joe and I shared a balcony together."

One day, Guidry said, he was standing on the balcony, smoking and listening to some rap music when Prystash came out to smoke a cigarette.

"We started talking about liking the same kind of music and started hanging out." They did not actually socialize in the true sense of the word, but grew friendlier in their balcony talks.

"Sometimes we would stay out on the balcony and have long conversations. Other times we would just say hello to each other. Joe would tell me how he made money beating people up and that he could make a lot of money doing it. Joe told me he had killed a man once for somebody and that he had made a lot of money."

Prystash harped on the money that could be made

in such strong-arming jobs. He asked Guidry if he would be interested in making some extra and easy money.

"I told him that I was, and Joe said he would get back to me."

Guidry continued: "About the first week in November of last year, me and Joe were out on the balcony talking. Joe told me that he had a friend that he worked out with and that he wanted his wife killed. I told him I really didn't want to be involved in any part of it.

"Joe told me that only a sucker wouldn't want to be involved for $500. And I said, 'What do I have to do for $500?' And Joe told me all I have to do is drive the car.

"I agreed to do it for $500."

Guidry was unaware of the skillful maneuvering by his older pal who "knew the business." Prystash was dangling the money bait and patiently waiting for Guidry to bite.

They met on the balcony to smoke two days later. Prystash told Guidry he was going to drive down to Atascocita and show him the neighborhood.

"I was going to be driving and I would drop him off on the same block that the house was located. This was the home of Joe's friend's wife that Joe was supposed to kill. Joe also told me that he was going to rape her first and kill her, and I was supposed to go back to the Food City [a nearby supermarket with outside pay phones] and wait for a phone call. I again asked him is that all I have to do is drive, and Joe said yes, and I would get paid as soon as I got back."

Guidry said that "about three days after we cut it up, Joe came out to the balcony and asked me, 'Are you ready to do it?' And I told him, 'Yes, I was.' "

Prystash told him they would wait until "nightfall" and "he wanted to get to her house before she got home."

Guidry recalled they left the apartment about 5:30 P.M. in Prystash's "older gray Nissan." Prystash drove when they left, explaining "he didn't want anyone to see me driving because it would look suspicious."

The suspect said they drove to Food City and tested the phones from Joe's cellular phone to make sure they worked.

They cased the house, and Guidry dropped him about twenty-five feet away, he said. Guidry went to wait by the pay phone at Food City, where Joe was to call when he was ready to be picked up. Finally Joe called and said, "I'm ready."

"When I picked him up, he was wearing all black clothes and was standing next to the fence.

"Joe jumped into the car and he was breathing real hard and he yelled for me to drive. Joe didn't say anything to me until we got up to Highway 1960. I asked if he did it and he said yes. Joe told me as soon as I got to the apartment, I was going to get paid.

"Joe made a call and then said he couldn't get the money until tomorrow. He told me it would be a while before I could get the money. He said the guy who was paying him was being questioned by police.

"I stayed up all night thinking about what he did."

Two weeks later when Guidry asked about his unpaid money, Prystash said he couldn't get it.

"I never did get paid for doing the job. I finally told Joe not to worry about it anymore because I didn't want to get into trouble. I forgot to say that he brought a black pistol with him the night that he killed that woman."

He said Prystash gave him the gun about four weeks after the murder.

"I put it up in my apartment."

Hoffman did not believe Guidry's statement. The detective was sure that Guidry was the shooter, not the driver. It was a gut feeling, but it was strong, and usually that gut instinct paid off for the homicide detective.

He read Guidry's statement. Then he told him he did not think it was true because of other pertinent facts he knew. He asked the suspect if he would take a lie detector test and Guidry agreed. Hoffman called Ernie Hulsey, the department's polygraph examiner, who came down and administered the test.

When it was done, Hulsey told Hoffman that the test showed the suspect was ninety-five percent deceptive in the confession he had given.

Hoffman and Hulsey explained the test results to Guidry, showing him the places in the statement where the lie detector chart indicated he was lying. There were a lot of places.

They kept talking to the suspect, quietly reiterating the case points from other evidence and witnesses that convinced them he was not telling the truth. Hoffman said there were indisputable witnesses who placed both Guidry and his buddy Prystash in the middle of the murder conspiracy.

Now, Hoffman added, they had the murder gun. Slugs test fired from the weapon had been compared to a slug found in the child's life preserver on the garage wall and found to match. They knew from phone records of the calls made from the church where Fratta had been with his kids that he was involved in the death plot and had set the killing into motion.

Finally, Guidry put his head in his hands and sat that way for a few seconds. Then he raised it and said he would make a second statement to clear up some things that were not accurate.

This time, Guidry "upped" it, as police parlance puts it.

EIGHTEEN

He began with an explanation:

"I'm making another statement because I want to clear up what happened. Everything was true in my first statement up until to where we started planning it. About two weeks in advance before the woman was killed, I was out on my apartment balcony talking to Joe Prystash.

"I was sitting there, and I told him, 'Man, I wish there was a way I could make some money.' He told me that he knew of a way I could make some big money. He told me that he was supposed to be taking care of this job. Joe told me he was supposed to take care of a friend's wife.

"I don't remember the exact words he used, but he meant to kill her. Joe said he didn't really want to do it because the guy was his friend and he knew the girl, too. Joe kept stressing that there was a lot of money involved.

"I asked how much, and he said $1,000 guaranteed after she was dead, and a Jeep and a couple of thousand in a few weeks. Joe said the guy was someone he worked out with. I said I would think about it.

"About three days before the woman was killed, Joe came back to the balcony and we talked about the plans of how it was going to go. It was the same plan as I told you before, except Joe said he was going to drive and I was to do the shooting. I did not plan it that way. Joe told me how he wanted it done.

"I don't remember the date the woman was killed. I met Joe that day on the balcony about 4 P.M.

"Joe asked if I was ready to do it, and I said, 'Sure.' Joe went in and ate, took a bath. Joe came back out about 5 P.M. or 5:30. Joe was saying she was fine and was saying she was so pretty. He said he wanted to rape her.

"Joe said her husband wanted to set her up by putting some dope in her purse. Joe said the husband wanted him to kill her and make it look like it was some kind of wild sex act.

"Joe said her husband wanted him to have sex with her and then choke her with a coat hanger. Joe then reminded me about when he broke into her house before. . . . Joe said he didn't take care of her then. Joe then gave me the gun, which was the same one I was arrested with. I think there was only four rounds in the gun, and they were .38s.

"I got in Joe's car, a gray Nissan two-door, and we drove up to Food City. Joe was wearing jeans and a dark-colored shirt. He was also wearing his glasses and his white tennis shoes.

"I was wearing a black T-shirt and some

black, khaki pants. Joe made a call from Mary's [Gibb] cellular phone. Joe paged her husband, and her husband paged him back with the number of the woman's house.

"I knew, because Joe told me that. Joe then called the woman's house, but nobody picked up the phone. I think the answering machine came on.

"Before that call to the woman's house, Joe paged the husband and her husband called Joe back.

"Joe had told me a week later that her husband called from a church where he was with his kids. Joe didn't tell me the husband's name, but when he tried paging him, Joe kept saying, 'Bob didn't call back.'

"Bob is the only name Joe said about the woman's husband. I forgot to say that Mary was the first call he made with the cellular phone. Joe was testing the phone then. Joe told her, 'I'm just testing the phone. I'll be home later. Love you.'

"Joe drove us to the neighborhood and he showed me where everything was at. He told me there was a baby house in the backyard and wanted me to get in it and wait for the woman to come. Joe gave me the cellular phone and showed me how to use it. We passed the front of the house twice.

"He was telling me what to do as we drove around the block. Joe dropped me off right in front of the house and drove off. I hopped a wooden fence and I got in a little house. I stayed in the little house for about an hour.

"The house was made of wood. I called Joe

on the cellular phone twice before the woman showed up. I called him at Food City. The first call, I said she wasn't here yet. He said to keep waiting. The second time I called, I told him the police kept passing.

"He said they always patrol around. I really didn't see no police. I just said that because I wanted to go. I went up to the back door and looked in the house. I thought she might have come home because I saw a light on. I saw nobody, so I went back to the little house.

"About ten minutes after that, a car pulled up in the garage. I heard it. I stood by the garage door that leads to the house. I heard some noise in the garage and finally someone opened the door that leads into the house. When she opened the door, I walked in the garage with the gun.

"She tried to give me her purse because she was scared. I shot her in the head and she fell. I shot her again in the head because she was still moving. I then ran back to the playhouse. When I shot her the first time, she fell forward towards her car. The second shot I just closed my eyes.

"I called Joe again and I told him to pick me up quick. Joe picked me up and asked how I did. He asked how she fell and if she was dead. I told him I didn't know, but just to get me back to the apartments. Joe kept rambling about me being his friend for life. Joe said he would have my money as soon as we got back.

"When we got back to the apartments, I went in my house and then came out on the balcony.

"Joe came out of his apartment and he said he couldn't get in touch with Bob. I told him 'whatever.' I told him I was going in my apartment and I was going to try to sleep. I gave Joe back the gun.

"The next day Joe told me that the night before he and his friend drove in his friend's truck past the house to see what the police were doing. Joe said the whole block was roped off with yellow tape.

"Joe gave me the pistol that day and I put it into my closet. Joe also said I couldn't get the money yet because Bob was being questioned by the police and he had the money on him. About three weeks to a month later Joe told me to dispose of the gun because he was being bothered by the police. He asked me if I had any friends who had a torch to cut the gun up. I said I didn't know anyone like that. He told me to throw the gun in the river and I said I would.

"I tried to give Joe back the gun, but he wouldn't take it. He said to dispose of it. Joe or Bob never paid me the money Joe said I would get."

The confession was signed Howard Paul Guidry and inscribed with the time: 1:09 A.M. (March 8, 1995).

The confessed killer was about to star in his own movie.

Riding in the car on their way to the filming location were Detective Sergeant Billingsley, Detectives

Hoffman, Bob Tonry and the admitted killer. They left the homicide office at 2:25 A.M., March 8.

After the confessions had been taken by Hoffman, Billingsley asked Guidry if he would do a walk-through reenactment of the murder. The suspect agreed.

First stopping to get a soft drink for Guidry, the detectives drove to the Vehicle Maintenance Center to get the car gassed up. Then they stopped at the District 2 Patrol Station at Humble to enlist the help of a uniformed deputy.

Billingsley wanted a uniformed officer with them so people in the neighborhood would know that all the post-midnight activity was on the up and up and not some Hollywood film crew that had wandered off the set.

Deputy Mitch Mehring accompanied the detectives. The deputy would provide the lighting with the headlights of his patrol car.

At the Davis Food City, Guidry walked over to one of two outside pay phones in front of the store and indicated the phone he and Prystash had checked by making a call to it from the cellular phone Guidry carried.

Then they drove a half mile to the Forest Fern residence where the victim had been shot.

Guidry went through the motions of climbing the fence behind the garage, then hiding in a large playhouse where he waited for Farah Fratta to come home. He demonstrated how he phoned from inside the playhouse to report that the woman had not showed up.

Guidry went through all of his actions of that night. The red light on the phone probably was the red glare the neighbor witnesses had seen when watching from across the street.

Hoffman narrated the video, explaining the various steps of murder that were reenacted by Guidry. It was like something out of a horror movie to watch as the suspect retraced his trail of murder.

When completed, the video was nineteen-minutes long.

NINETEEN

Early on, Danny Billingsley wanted to be a law-enforcement officer. Graduating from high school in 1964, he joined the Air Force and served four years, including one year in Vietnam as an engineer. He attended Sam Houston University where he received a bachelor's degree in police science and he added thirty hours toward a master's degree in that field. During his college study, he was an intern with the Harris County Sheriff's Department. That led to his employment by the department as a deputy in 1988. He was assigned to the homicide division in 1990 and later was promoted to detective and then detective sergeant.

At six feet, 200 pounds, with blue eyes and graying hair, he had the physical bearing for the job. People trusted him—the good guys and the bad guys.

On the same day that Howard Guidry had given his confession and reenactment of the crime, Billingsley and his homicide cohorts planned to arrest the suspected middle man in the murder conspiracy, Joe Prystash.

Prystash was staying with his father at Conroe, in neighboring Montgomery County, Texas. Billingsley had assigned detectives to surveillance of the father's house, to tail Prystash when he left that morning.

The surveillance team would notify Billingsley when Prystash crossed into Harris County. It would simplify procedural matters to arrest him in Harris County.

Billingsley and Detective Bob Tonry were waiting for the call from the detectives following Prystash. Unfortunately, they lost Prystash in heavy traffic. Luckily, Billingsley happened to spot him after he had entered the county.

The detectives followed him to the Red Lobster Restaurant on Highway 59, just north of FM 1960. When he parked in front, Billingsley and Tonry left their unit and walked toward him. Prystash recognized them and stopped by his car.

Billingsley advised Prystash that they had a warrant for his arrest in the murder of Farah Fratta. It was a "pocket warrant," which allowed the arrested subject to be held a maximum of twenty-four hours. Detective Ronnie Roberts had obtained the warrant earlier from the district attorney's office and took it to a magistrate to sign.

It was 4:20 P.M. when the arrest was made and Prystash was taken to the homicide office for questioning.

Over the next hour and a half, Tonry questioned him, but Prystash wasn't talking. He denied any involvement in the murder. No, he did not wish to make a voluntary statement or any other kind.

During the evening, Prystash told Billingsley that he would make a statement if he could go home first to tend to some business.

Billingsley phoned Assistant District Attorney Dan

Rizzo and related the suspect's offer to talk if allowed the home visit.

Rizzo turned thumbs down on the proposition. If a statement were taken after granting the request, it would amount to coercion and invalidate anything the suspect might say, Rizzo pointed out.

The pocket warrant's time for holding a suspect was already running down. It wouldn't do any good to keep him in jail overnight if he wasn't going to talk to the detectives. Billingsley decided to cut him loose and get a new warrant.

It was 9:20 P.M. when Billingsley left with Prystash to drive him back to his car parked at the restaurant where he had been nabbed.

On the way, Prystash asked if they could stop and let him get cigarettes. Billingsley pulled into a convenience store at Lockwood and Clinton. Prystash went alone to get the cigarettes and a soft drink.

The two men were silent as they drove through the darkness.

"Are we being followed?" Prystash asked. He was referring to another sheriff's unit.

Billingsley looked at his passenger and shook his head.

"No, we're not being followed," he said.

Prystash asked Billingsley how long he had been an officer and if he liked his job.

"Yes, I usually like my job," Billingsley said.

Prystash asked if Billingsley was wearing a recording device.

Billingsley said he was not wired.

He pulled his unit up beside the suspect's car. Prystash said his keys had not been working right lately and asked if Billingsley would mind waiting until he made sure his car started.

Billingsley nodded. He had the impression that Prystash was stalling, trying to make up his mind about something.

"Are you going to arrest me tonight?" Prystash asked.

Billingsley replied no, adding it would be several days probably.

Prystash glanced around the area. Here it comes, the detective thought.

"Do you have a coat?" Prystash asked.

"Yeah, it's in the back seat. Why?"

"We need to take a walk," Prystash said.

What's this guy up to? Billingsley wondered. He felt he could handle him. He reached for his coat and got out. The night was cool for Houston. They started walking toward the rear of the parking lot.

"You sure you don't have a recorder?"

Billingsley opened his coat, holding the sides away from his body.

Suddenly Prystash patted him down, like a cop does when making an arrest. Billingsley could not believe it. This guy was something else.

They walked on a short distance. Prystash sighed and said, "Well, you have it about right. It happened about like you think."

He continued, "Like a lot of other people, Bob approached me about having his wife killed. And he asked me if I knew someone who could do it, and I told him I probably did. He offered me $1,000 and the Jeep he owned."

Later on, Bob approached him again and said, "I can find someone to do it with you."

Joe said he had told Fratta, "No, I'll take care of that myself."

Prystash said he made contact with Howard Guidry

sometime after that. He said Fratta had given him a schedule of his wife's daily activities and also a gun.

Prystash related that on November 9 he took Guidry to her house and returned to the Food City to wait for Guidry's call when he finished.

"When he called, I picked him up and we went back to our apartments."

He said Fratta never paid him the promised money.

Prystash said he had "got away from Howard Guidry after the killing because he "did not like Guidry around Mary Gipp and Guidry talked about illegal things he was involved in."

After his off-the-cuff confession, Prystash asked Billingsley, "What do you want to do?"

The homicide sergeant knew there was nothing he could do at this point, considering what the assistant D.A. had told him.

But Billingsley said, "Well, I would like to take a statement off of you."

Prystash only responded with another question. "How much time do you think I'll get out of this?"

Billingsley said he could not make any promises. That would have to be discussed with the district attorney's office. But he did say that in his opinion, the driver was the only one who might be able to deal in this case.

Billingsley told Prystash that he would take him to visit with the D.A.'s people tomorrow and they could talk about it.

"I have a test tomorrow," said Prystash (he was attending a mechanics school). "I'll call you when I get through with that."

Billingsley gave him one of his cards. Before they parted, Prystash asked if Billingsley thought he needed an attorney.

"If I told you you didn't need an attorney, you would know I was lying to you. Sooner or later, you're going to need an attorney."

"Well, all they want is money anyway," said Prystash.

Billingsley wondered if he had done the right thing in letting the guy walk. He shrugged. There wasn't anything else he could do, under the legal circumstances involved.

But he was not much surprised when he did not hear from Prystash the next day.

Billingsley issued orders to get a new warrant and bring him in. As it turned out, finding Prystash was not all that cut and dried. Again the detective sergeant wasn't surprised.

One of the detectives had heard that Prystash was keeping company with an attractive schoolteacher. The suspect had made himself scarce as far as the premises of Mary Gipp were concerned.

But less than a week after Prystash was turned loose, Billingsley's detective squad was setting up a trap for Joe Prystash. The date was March 13, 1995. They had a new warrant, and they were eager to serve it.

Detective Larry Davis was in his unit parked near an elementary school in the vicinity of Beltway 8 and Highway 59. He and Detective Valerio, in another car, were waiting for Prystash's teacher friend to leave in hopes she would lead them to the elusive suspect.

Davis saw the teacher's automobile pull away from the school and turn east on Beltway.

The deputies followed her off of Wilson Road to a bowling alley, where she turned down a dead-end road. Davis stayed behind her. He kept going straight to a road that ran adjacent behind the road where the teacher was driving.

He tried to reach Valerio on the radio, but could not raise him.

He assumed Valerio probably had switched to the primary channel, a channel on which officers in marked units can be contacted. On the primary channel he heard Valerio giving his location.

Davis went back down Wilson Road to Beltway and saw Valerio and a car occupied by Prystash on the right shoulder of the road, near Highway 59. Deputy McGruin also was there.

When Davis pulled up, Valerio told him that Prystash had been placed under arrest.

Prystash was placed in a marked patrol car for the ride to the homicide office.

Davis headed back to his office and arrived in time to see Prystash being escorted inside.

Sergeant Billingsley told Davis to take Prystash to the processing center on Commerce. It was about 7:10 P.M. Davis and Valerio, with Prystash in tow, headed for Davis's unit. When the detectives came out of the door, it looked like every news media outlet in Houston was there.

When the newspeople spotted Prystash, they closed in, making it difficult for the detectives and the suspect to get through. The reporters and photographers crowded around Prystash, sticking microphones and cameras in his face. Questions came from every direction, such as "Are you the murderer?"

Prystash was getting mad.

At the processing center, Davis pulled up to the sally port area. It was necessary to honk to have the door opened from inside, and there was not an immediate response.

As they waited to get inside, Prystash asked, "What's going to happen to Bob [Fratta]?" Davis said they could not talk about that.

"We need to go talk," Prystash said.

Davis turned around to go back to the homicide office. Prystash was worried about getting through the news media mob again. Davis told him to lie down in the backseat, and instead of returning to where they had first taken him out, Davis drove around to the front door of the homicide office on the other side of the building.

Another detective met them there, and he and Valerio took Prystash inside while Davis parked his unit.

Prystash now was wanting to make a statement. They led him to an interview room. Inside were two chairs and a gray typing stand. Davis seated Prystash, and Valerio came in with his laptop computer. Valerio brought up a personal custody form on the screen and from that read to the suspect his legal rights.

Prystash asked for a Coke, and one of the detectives went to get it. He said he was hungry and a pizza was ordered and delivered. Also a pack of cigarettes. After Prystash waived his right to have an attorney present, Valerio began taking the statement.

The interrogation was interrupted several times for Prystash to go to the bathroom.

When the statement was completed, the suspect was told to read and initial each paragraph of his confession if it was correct, which he did.

Guidry in his confession had said he knew the man who wanted his wife killed only as "Bob." Prystash had never mentioned Bob's last name to the trigger-man, according to Guidry.

Now the detectives had a confession in which Bob Fratta was named as the one who initiated the mur-der-for-hire.

TWENTY

Sergeant Billingsley came into the interview room to witness Prystash's signing of the self-incriminating statement.

The three-page confession, dated March 13, 1995, at 7:22 P.M., read as follows:

"My full name is Joseph Andrew Prystash and I am a white male, 38 years of age. I was born on 09-05-56, in Youngstown, Ohio. I reside in Conroe, TX with my father.

"On March 13, 1995, at approximately 4:25 P.M., I was in a meeting at the District Attorney's Office with Assistant District Attorney Dan Rizzo and Sgt. Danny Billingsley. Prior to talking to me, Rizzo read me my legal warnings. I told him that I understood each part. He then asked me if I wished to talk to him about the case or ask any questions about the case. At this time, I told him that I wanted a lawyer.

"The meeting was stopped, and Sgt. Billingsley took me and had me fingerprinted and then I was taken to the homicide office. Later that evening, Detective Valerio and Detective

Davis were taking me to jail. Before arriving at the jail, I told them that we needed to talk.

"We then returned to the homicide office, and I agreed to give them a statement about what had happened.

"About a month before Farah Fratta was killed, I was working out at the President and First Lady in Humble. As I worked out, Bob Fratta walked by me. (I had known Bob Fratta for six or seven years from the gym. I knew that he was a police officer in Missouri City.) He said hello, and we talked for a few minutes. The last thing he said before he walked out was, 'Do you know anybody that would kill my wife for me?' I believe I told him that I might know somebody.

"Bob told me that he was willing to pay $1,000 to the killer after the killing. Bob told me that he could come up with a lot more after the killing. He told me that he was going to give me the Jeep for me to sell. After the Jeep was sold, I was to give the money to the person I hired.

"Bob told me that he could give the killer payments until he got up to around $5,000. I told him that I would get back to him.

"I met Howard Guidry a short time after I talked with Bob about killing his wife. He lived in the apartment next to mine . . . Howard told me that he needed to make some money and he didn't care what he did. He said that he wanted to move out of his sister's apartment.

"Shortly after I met Howard I asked him if he was willing to kill Farah Fratta. He told me that he was willing. I told him that Bob was willing to pay $1,000 and more money later.

"Howard was interested right from the beginning because he wanted to go buy some cocaine, and sell it.

"Between the first and the second meeting, Bob Fratta and I talked on the telephone several times. We arranged a sccond meeting at Wyatt's Cafeteria in Humble. The second time we met was at Wyatt's Cafeteria about a week later. Bob drew maps of Farah's neighborhood on a napkin for me. He showed me how to get to her house from the front of her neighborhood. We talked about several scenarios. One of the scenarios involved rolling up beside a stop sign by Farah's baby sitter's house and shooting Farah. Bob told me that the killer would have to take something from her to make it look like a robbery.

"Another scenario involved going to her job, in an office in the Galeria area. He wanted the killer to shoot her in the office or in the parking area. He talked about how this parking lot was real long and went into a parking area. Again he wanted it to look like a robbery or a drug deal. He told me that she works in a Marriott hotel. He said that she would occasionally work at another office in the Greenspoint area. Bob wanted me to give the killer all the ideas and let him make up his mind. Bob understood from the beginning that I wasn't going to do it.

"At one point Bob told me that he had another guy set up to do the killing. He asked me if I wanted him to help. I told him 'No.'

"Bob told me that if I got caught, I should tell the police that Farah paid me to hurt her so that he would get the blame.

"I left several messages for Bob on his answering machine. We met at his house about a week before Farah was killed. Bob told me that he wanted Farah killed when his kids weren't with his wife.

"About a week before the killing Bob and I met and he told me that he was going to be at church the following Wednesday night. He said that the following Wednesday night would be perfect because he'd have his kids until 9 P.M. He told me that he was going to have an extra hour of visitation because he was taking the kids to church. I didn't know what church he was going to be at. Bob had told me that he had visitation every Wednesday between, like, 6 P.M. until 8 P.M.

"About three days before Farah was killed, Bob came up to where I go to school, at UTL, and gave me a gun to give to Howard. The gun was a blue Police Bulldog Special revolver with what was probably a 4″ barrel. The gun had brown real wood grips. The gun was in a soft gun case with fur on the inside. The outside of the case was black plastic. He also gave me a box of .38 special bullets. I think the box was green and yellow. The bullets were lead and had sort of flat tops. They weren't hollow points. The casings were silver. Bob had told me before that day that he had a gun or a knife for Howard to use.

"Howard had decided that he wanted to use the gun. I had told Bob that Howard wanted the gun and a box of shells. Bob also gave me $25 to give to Howard. Howard had told me that he wanted the money for some 'AMP.'

"AMP is like an embalming fluid that you dip marijuana in to make it more potent. I asked Howard what it does and he told me that you can do anything on your mind when you're on it.

"The day of the killing, Howard's sister was gone with her car. (Howard had planned to use her car.) I had my dad's car. My dad's car was a 1991 cherry-colored Chrysler New Yorker Fifth Avenue. Howard asked me if I would drive. I told him that I would. He was having a problem finding someone to drive him. I gave him my cell phone and told him to call me after he shot Farah.

"I took Howard over to the parking lot of the Food City at . . . East Timber Forest. We got there about 7:30 P.M.. At about 7:35 I got a page from Bob. I called him back with either the store pay phone or the mobile phone. Bob told me that he was at church. I told him that Howard was ready to go. Bob said, 'All right.' After I got off the phone with Bob, I drove Howard to Farah's house. I dropped him off a few houses away from Farah's house. (I knew where to go because of the map Bob gave me.) I believe I dropped him off shortly before 8 P.M. After I left Howard I went back to the Food City and waited by the pay phones. Howard called me about 7:55 P.M. He told me that she wasn't home yet.

"I paged Bob and he called me back. Bob told me, 'Wait, she'll be there.' I told him 'okay' and hung up the phone. Maybe five seconds later I got another call on the mobile phone.

"Howard told me, 'Come and get me fast.' He was kind of out of breath.

"I hung up the phone and drove to Farah's house. Howard was on the side of the garage. He came out and got into the front passenger-side door. I saw that the garage door was open and the light was off. I couldn't see inside the garage.

"I could see a white car backed in the garage. The car might have had a red emblem on the front. After Howard got back into the car he told me that he came up to her by her car on the driver's side of her car, and she stepped away from him. He said that she told him, 'Please don't kill me.' He said that he shot her in the head and she fell down.

"He said that she was making noise so he shot her again in the head. He didn't tell me where in the head that he shot her.

"After I left Farah's house, I drove out of the subdivision and back west on FM 1960 towards my apartment. Shortly before or after we got back to my apartment, I got a call from Bob. I told him that his wife had been killed. He told me that he would meet me at the gym at 9 P.M.

"After Howard and I got out of the car, I took the gun from the car. (Howard had left it in the car). I picked up the gun and took it into my apartment. I took it into my bedroom and took all the shells out of it. I put the shells in the kitchen garbage. After that I took the gun over to Howard's apartment and gave him the gun. I told him that he should get rid of it.

"Howard told me that he was going to throw it into a lake or something. After that I went to the President and First Lady in Humble. Bob never showed up.

"The next night I saw the news and saw why Bob did not show up. I saw that he was going somewhere with the police.

"The next evening, after Bob got out of jail, Bob called me. He told me that the police had confiscated the money he was going to pay Howard with. After I talked with Bob, I had to tell Howard that he wasn't going to get his money for a while.

"As time went on, Howard got real mad about not getting paid. I told him that I would tell him where Bob lived and where he worked out, but he never asked for the information.

"I tried to help Howard get his money a few times. Bob kept putting me off. I wanted to get Howard off my back. Howard and I never got any money from Bob.

"I've been depressed ever since this happened. I didn't sleep a lot of nights because I felt bad about it. Bob called me several times after it happened to find out if my girlfriend Mary Gipp knew anything. I was afraid that Bob might hurt Mary by getting her involved. I didn't want Mary to have anything to do with the whole situation."

On March 30, 1995, Lex Baquer read in the newspaper that the sheriff's department had recovered the gun with which Farah Fratta had been killed.

The news report struck a chord in Baquer's memory.

From the description of the gun, it sounded like a weapon he was very familiar with. Baquer put down the paper and phoned Casey O'Brien of the district attorney's office. He knew that O'Brien was working on the murder case.

He asked what caliber of gun was used in his daughter's death.

O'Brien told him it was a .38-caliber revolver.

"I think I may know that gun," Baquer said.

O'Brien told him to call the sheriff's department and talk to Sergeant Dan Billingsley.

The next day, Baquer decided to go personally to the sheriff's department. He asked for Sergeant Billingsley.

"I thought instead of calling, I would come in and maybe I could see that gun," Baquer said.

Billingsley asked Baquer to describe the gun.

He described a .38-caliber revolver that he thought his daughter had given to him for safekeeping. He told the sergeant the gun was a revolver and did not have a safety device and had a brown handle.

The sergeant asked him if he could draw the gun. Baquer made a sketch and Billingsley studied it a moment.

"Will you wait in my office please?" Billingsley said and stepped out.

After about fifteen minutes, Baquer was escorted into a room down the corridor. He saw a table with several guns lined up on it. The gun lineup had been prepared by Detective Larry Davis.

Suddenly Baquer felt sick. He recognized the gun immediately.

He asked Davis, "Can I pick it up?" and the detective said yes. He gingerly lifted the gun and turned it over and then back again.

"Yes, I recognize this gun," Baquer said emotionally.

The last time he had seen it was in the summer of 1994, Baquer recalled. He had had it in his possession since 1993.

One day when she returned from work, Farah Fratta was told by her baby sitter that Bradley had found a gun in the house. The mother recognized it when she saw it. It was a gun that Bob Fratta had bought for her in 1982 for her protection. That was a year before they were married, when both of them were working for American Airlines.

Farah had forgotten all about the gun being in the house. She called her father and said, "Dad, will you take this gun. I don't want a gun in the house."

Lex Baquer had picked up the gun and had it since that time.

Then one day his daughter called him and said Bob had asked for the gun. Baquer said he would give him the gun at the first opportunity.

Fratta came to the Baquer residence on a Saturday. He drove in the driveway with the three Fratta children about 6 P.M., returning them from their regular visitation.

Baquer gave him the revolver in its gun case, several boxes of ammunition and some loose bullets that were in the gun case.

Only a few months later, a killer would use the same gun to shoot Farah Fratta down—the gun that ironically had been bought for her protection more than a decade before.

Much later, homicide detectives conjectured that Bob Fratta must have relished that moment when he passed along the gun to Joe Prystash to give to Howard Guidry

They thought Fratta was a guy who enjoyed special little touches like that.

TWENTY-ONE

Both Howard Guidry and Joseph Prystash were in jail on charges of capital murder.

The investigators were wrapping up their case against Bob Fratta. They had the murder weapon. Test-fired bullets from the gun matched the one comparable slug recovered at the crime scene. They had Lex Baquer's testimony that he had given the gun to Fratta at his daughter's request a few months before the slaying. They had the confession of Prystash fingering Fratta as the instigator of the killing. They had witnesses that Fratta had been trying to hire a killer for months before it happened.

They had Guidry's confession of how he put two bullets in the victim's head.

They had Mary Gipp's damning statement of Prystash's return to the apartment after the murder and what he told her and did. They had the phone records to and from the cellular phone carried by the shooter, with calls linked to the church where Fratta had used the phone.

They had everything except Bob Fratta under arrest, and on April 21, 1995, they were about to do that.

* * *

For nearly a month, up until the day before Fratta's arrest, Casey O'Brien had been trying to make a deal with Prystash, offering him a more lenient sentence in exchange for his testimony against Fratta.

Prystash at first agreed to testify against Fratta for a sentence of fifty to fifty-five years in prison, but then he backed out; he had said he wouldn't flip over, even if the state offered him as little as three years in prison.

O'Brien told him, "Okay, you don't have to, but I'm going to make sure that you die."

By now, the prosecutors and detectives believed they had sufficient evidence to convict Fratta without the testimony of either Prystash or Guidry.

The district attorney's office had given the go-ahead, and the arrest warrant on a charge of solicitation of murder was issued.

Not only were they certain they could nail Fratta, the prosecutors were considering upgrading the solicitation charge to capital murder, which was punishable by death.

"Well, let's go get him," Sergeant Billingsley said. Besides Billingsley, the investigators who headed to Fratta's residence in northeast Houston shortly before 5:30 P.M. on that Friday included Sergeant John Denholm, Detectives James Hoffman, Ronnie Roberts, Harry Fikaris and William Valerio. All had worked long hours on the case and looked forward to making the long-wanted collar of the smug-faced body-builder.

They walked to the door and rang the bell. It was Fratta's mother from New York who came to the door. She was advised that they had a warrant for the arrest of Bob Fratta. When the detectives entered, they saw Fratta walking toward them from the dining room area.

"What's going on?" he asked sharply.

"You are under arrest on a charge of solicitation of murder," one detective responded.

Hoffman took Fratta by the arm and prepared to handcuff him. Fratta said he did not want to be handcuffed in front of his mother and tried to jerk free. With Hoffman the first detective to make contact, he and several other detectives wrestled Fratta to the floor and handcuffed him behind his back.

His mother was restrained as the brief struggle ensued.

The suspect was taken to the homicide office. When his legal rights were read to him, Fratta said he had nothing to say.

As he was taken from the homicide office by Roberts and Hoffman to be booked into jail, the waiting news media closed in. Fratta, handcuffed and wearing ankle chains, said, "I didn't do it. I'm praying for justice."

He was held in jail with bond denied.

It had been nearly six and one-half months since that night of November 9, 1994 when he was first questioned by Detective Valerio. Fratta was not smirking this time.

On Friday, June 2, 1995, all three of the suspects were indicted by a Harris County grand jury on charges of capital murder. The instigator, the middle man and the shooter now faced possible death sentences.

The cases were on file in the 230th State District,

a court that is one of several in Division C of the district attorney's office. Each division has a senior prosecutor with the primary responsibility for all capital cases filed in that court.

Thus Assistant District Attorney Kelly Siegler was designated as the lead attorney in the Fratta, Prystash and Guidry cases.

Which suited Assistant District Attorney Casey O'Brien, the Division C chief, just fine. "Kelly may be the best trial lawyer in the office," he said. "She is fabulous."

O'Brien himself, who recently had been transferred to the position of Division C trial bureau chief over all the courts in that division, would be second lawyer in the Fratta and the other two cases. As division trial bureau chief, his job was to supervise and assist the prosecutors of the division in major cases.

O'Brien was no slouch himself when it came to trying a capital case. The veteran of over twenty-two years in the D.A.'s office was known for his toughness and tenacity and even histrionics when merited. And he had an Irish sense of humor.

At the time the Fratta case was under investigation, O'Brien was working some with the special crimes unit of the D.A.'s office. So he already was partly familiar with the Fratta case.

The order in which the three murder cases should be tried was the subject of some discussion. Siegler believed strongly that Bob Fratta, as the one responsible for ordering his wife's murder, should go on trial first. The mother of three children would be alive if he had not hired a killer.

"I think the thing that most people were surprised

about is that I made the decision that we were going to try Fratta's case first. And most people would have thought we would try the shooter first. But it just seemed to me more appropriate that we should try Bob Fratta's case first because if the man responsible for Farah being killed didn't get the death penalty, it kind of put the other ones in a different perspective. And I felt like a jury would hear all the evidence and just think he deserves the death penalty."

The shooter, although also deserving of death, had been Fratta's mechanism to accomplish his purpose.

As for Prystash, the assistant district attorney considered him to be in a category by himself. As she explained her theory:

"I think Joe Prystash is cold-blooded. I think Bob Fratta did it because he's selfish and vain and conceited and thinks the world revolves around him. I think Howard Guidry did it because he's stupid; he had a crack problem and he didn't think.

"But I think Joe Prystash is a scary, sociopathic killer. He didn't have any reason to get involved. He didn't need to help. He just wanted to help. And why? He is sick. To me that was the most telling thing about Prystash. He just did it because he liked doing it."

O'Brien supported Siegler's belief that Fratta should be first up.

Both of the experienced prosecutors wanted the death penalty for all three defendants, but District Attorney John Holmes had to give his approval first, as was customary in all capital cases tried by the D.A.'s office.

Siegler and O'Brien met with Holmes to lay out the evidence and their intention of seeking the maximum verdict for the three murder defendants. There had been concern by other attorneys in the office that there wasn't sufficient evidence against Fratta.

Siegler and O'Brien and the police detectives thought there was plenty to proceed with.

Holmes agreed, too, that there was ample evidence and it justified the death penalty.

Holmes looked like an old-time Western gunfighter with his handlebar mustache twirled up at the ends. Since he became district attorney in 1979, the fiery D.A. and his prosecutors had sent 134 men and women to Texas's death row. Not another county in Texas had a tougher stance on the death penalty than Harris County.

And that was because of the strong-willed Holmes, who some observers had said thought more like a peace officer than a district attorney.

The *Houston Chronicle* ran a story on the district attorney's controversial attitude about the death penalty, saying, "To his detractors, Holmes is an inflexible and stubborn prosecutor perpetually lost in the third reel of a John Wayne movie."

As Holmes once explained about seeking the maximum penalty, "That decision is mine unilaterally. Every chief prosecutor who handles a capital case comes to me for formalization for whether or not they're seeking death, and I either agree with them or I disagree with them. Go out there and see if you can find any one person I've disagreed with.

"But, yes, I make the call because when it comes to testifying on appeal, I don't want there to be twenty-two different versions. I want there to be one. And that's me."

* * *

The only reason that Kelly Siegler could give for going to the University of Texas and studying international business was that it was a case of a hick desperate to get out of a small town.

The tiny town of Blessing, Texas, in Matagorda County, was full of friendly and caring people. And Siegler gave credit to the easygoing lifestyle, and those small-town relationships where everybody knows everyone else, for making it easier to relate to people of the big city when she moved there.

She graduated in three years from the University of Texas with the degree in international business. While in high school, she had thought about law school and a career in law. She was not sure why. She did not know any lawyers. In fact, there were not many lawyers in Matagorda County. But she opted for international business and dreamed of traveling the world as a big-time corporate lawyer. The trouble was, she needed a law degree to do that.

She enrolled in South Texas University at Houston and obtained a law degree in 1987. During her last year, she had worked as an intern for the Harris County District Attorney's office. When she found out a friend was quitting the staff, she applied and got the job.

She was first assigned to the family criminal law division. She went from that job to the county court as the No. 3 prosecutor, bottom on the totem pole, handling misdemeanor cases. Over the years she rose up the ranks to the felony division.

From the beginning, she knew she had found her niche. Criminal law was by far more interesting than the boring civil stuff. She found that her early life in Blessing made it easier to know and relate to people when picking juries, talking to witnesses, getting the cops to like her.

Now, as the top gun in 230th District Court, she braced herself for three more death penalty cases. She already had tried eight and had obtained seven death sentences. The other case ended in a hung jury and the defendant pleaded guilty in return for a life sentence.

Not a bad record at all for the small-town girl who had grown up to be one of the best and toughest capital murder prosecutors to hit Johnny Holmes–land in a long time.

She had developed a different outlook on the death penalty as punishment. A jury had to answer such questions as "Will the defendant be a continuing threat to society?" but she was not sure the jurors based their verdict on the answer.

She still thought capital punishment was necessary because Texas did not have a "life without parole" law. In many cases, the death penalty was the only solution.

But she also thought that if there were a life without parole statute, then the death penalty would not be needed as often.

Yet—and she firmly believed this—there would always be those defendants for whom killing them was the only solution. To her way of thinking, there were defendants "who just flat out deserved to die." It was a popular concept, too, of veteran homicide investigators who had been through the horrors and nightmares and seen the everlasting sorrow and grief of victims' families that a heinous crime can leave engraved on the human mind forever.

"However much we want to pretend that it doesn't mean this, really what it comes down to most of the time is that juries just vote with their gut and with their heart and say this defendant just deserves it"—the continuing threat to society and all the other legal excuses for putting them to death aside.

Kelly Siegler, preparing to try the three accused killers in the murder of Farah Fratta, believed the three defendants fell in that classification that no advocate of capital punishment wants to publicly talk about—"they just flat out deserved to die."

She and coprosecutor Casey O'Brien got down to the planning of a well-organized presentation of evidence that would give jurors an opportunity to exercise their death-dealing power.

TWENTY-TWO

Kelly Siegler sat in the office across the hall from her own office, studying the files spread over the floor. She was in that office because she needed more room. There was a file for each witness who would testify in Bob Fratta's murder trial, about forty files in all.

Preparing for trial, she had talked personally to each one of the witnesses, having traveled over the country to contact some of them. She had been on the phone with other witnesses until her arm felt as if it would drop off.

She did not sleep all that well at night, either, because her mind always was on the trial plan. Now sitting in the office, plotting the trial strategy, she could see no end to the work that already had been overwhelming.

Siegler made the decision on which of the witnesses would be examined by each of the prosecutors. She knew that Mary Gipp would be assigned to O'Brien. She and Gipp had had a clash of personalities during a pretrial interview, and there was no way she could successfully question the witness.

Siegler had accused Gipp of not answering the interview questions truthfully.

Gipp had said, "I don't have to put up with this."

"You damn well do have to put up with it," Siegler replied, and the conversation went downhill from there.

So it would be up to O'Brien to take Mary Gipp through testimony that was vital to the prosecution.

Siegler would question most of the police officers and some of the civilian witnesses whom she had talked to preparing for trial. Although Gipp would be an important witness in the Fratta trial, Siegler saw the trial plan as a "connect the dots" sort of thing, tying together many little pieces of related evidence and nailing Fratta's church alibi to the wall.

She would prove to the jury that although Fratta was at the church with his children, he was in touch by phone with the middleman Prystash, who in turn was in phone contact with the shooter. Fratta had been very much in control of the murder of his wife.

To Siegler, the diabolical plan of murder was one of the most cold-blooded she had seen. What kind of a father would order the mother of his three children shot to death and then plan to have the children with him when he "discovered" her bloody body in the garage?

Bob Fratta's capital murder trial began on April 9, 1996, in the tall building on San Jacinto Street that housed the criminal district courts, but not all of them by any means. Harris County long ago had outgrown its available courtroom facilities. Makeshift courtrooms had been set up in an old fire station and in a former theater, to mention only two.

Visiting outside judges, retired from their own courtroom benches but still working, came to Houston regularly to augment the resident district judges swamped by burgeoning case loads.

The District Attorneys Building was located on South Fannin, a block east of the Criminal Courts Building. Every morning of a trial, the state prosecutors walked a block from their building to the courts building.

Known judges and lawyers were passed automatically by the security officers manning the busy security barrier in the lobby of the courts building. Long lines of witnesses and spectators and other people there on business daily flooded the security area starting at 7:30 or 8 A.M.

The point of entry in the lobby was as busy as the security gates of a large airport.

On this morning of beginning testimony, Assistant District Attorneys Kelly Siegler and Casey O'Brien were seated at the counsel table in 230th District Court. On the other side of the table were Fratta's lawyers, two of the top-rated defense attorneys of Houston: Michael Charlton and John Ackerman. Presiding in the trial was visiting Judge Bob Burdette.

Handcuffs and ankle chains were removed from the defendant before he was brought into the courtroom.

When court was gaveled into session, the indictment against Robert Alan Fratta was read aloud. He stood up and entered a plea of not guilty.

Prosecutor Siegler rose to give the state's opening statement.

She began, "Ladies and gentlemen, the evidence will show you throughout the course of this week and through the testimony of approximately forty witnesses about the tragedy that happened to Farah Fratta on November 9, 1994.

"You will come to know through the evidence,

through the testimony of friends and acquaintances and employees who worked with him what this man is all about."

She related to the jury the possible motives that led to Fratta's hiring a killer to murder his wife: a large amount of money from a life insurance policy on his wife in which Fratta mistakenly thought he was the named beneficiary; dissatisfaction with his sexual life as it was in their marriage; and anger over his wife's public disclosure in a deposition related to the divorce suit of his revolting, repulsive and deviant sexual demands made during their marriage.

Siegler told the jury the capital murder charge against Fratta would be supported with telephone records, ballistics reports, and testimony of numerous witnesses. She pointed out that during the long and bitterly contested divorce-child custody suit, the defendant frequently made threatening remarks such as, "She will never divorce me. She's mine. I'm not going to let some other man have what I paid for." (Referring in part to breast implant surgery his wife underwent at his request.)

Summing up, Siegler said, "At the conclusion of all the evidence in this case, you are going to hear that this defendant never showed any remorse, never shed a tear, and was never sad at the execution of the mother of his three children . . . you are going to know that this defendant committed this capital murder for money because he wasn't going to let her beat him by divorcing him, because of his hatred for her and because she humiliated him by what she said to them in that deposition and, based on all the evidence you will hear in this case, you will have no reasonable doubt that this defendant is guilty of murder."

* * *

Called as the state's opening witness was Farah Fratta's first attorney in her divorce-custody case, James Beeler. The lawyer said he was hired in March 1992 and filed her divorce suit. He had talked with Bob Fratta several times about matters in the divorce.

Siegler questioned the witness. Beeler recalled Fratta wanted to be joint managing conservator. Farah agreed to all of Fratta's terms except his designation as joint managing conservator. She wanted to be the managing conservator, but she didn't have any objection to his having equal access to the children, or to any of the medical or school records or anything.

Q. The way the law stood in 1994, can you tell us that if the title had been given to Bob Fratta of joint managing conservator along with Farah Fratta and something had happened to either one of them, if they died or whatever, what would happen legally as far as the rights of the one who survived?

A. Basically, the survivor would become the sole managing conservator of those children.

Q. Let's talk about the financial situation, Mr. Beeler. The three children, Bradley, Daniel and Amber, was there any money in trust for them back in 1994?

A. There was.

Q. About how much was it?

A. It was over $100,000. It was in a foreign bank account.

Q. If Bob Fratta had been given the title of joint managing conservator and something had happened to Farah Fratta, what would have happened and who would have control of the money?

A. Bob Fratta.

Q. Would Lex and Betty Baquer as the grand-parents of the children have had an opportunity to try and get the children if he would have been named joint managing conservator?

A. They would have had to file a separate cause by action under grandparents' access, and you know, as the law applied, they would not have stood much chance of getting access to the children.

Concerning discussions he had with Fratta, the lawyer said, "He was quite open and frank about the condition of his marriage and what he expected. Basically Bob Fratta wanted an 'open marriage.' He wanted other women. He wanted other women along with Farah, two women at the same time. This was quote, the straw that broke the camel's back, and is why she filed."

Q. Did he ever speak to you about his satisfaction with their sex life?

A. Right. He talked about his sex life, not their sex life.

Q. What did he say?

A. Well, basically, that there wasn't enough excitement.

Q. Basically, what did Bob Fratta tell you about their sex life?

A. Basically, he told me that he wanted other women. He made a point of boasting in his openness about other women that he had been with.

Beeler testified that when he filed the legal action for Farah Fratta, it was a "fault" divorce. He said that he, Farah, her husband and his lawyer and a court reporter got together in December 1993 for each of the divorce parties to give depositions in preparation for the divorce trial later.

Q. Up to the time of the depositions, had anybody yet brought up the reasons for the 'fault' divorce?

A. No.

Q. On that day did it get brought up?

A. It did.

Q. Who brought it up?

A. Fratta's attorney.

Q. Did Farah answer him?

A. Well, she told him her definition—she turned to him and told him that Bob Fratta wanted her to defecate in his face, to urinate in his face, to choke him while he was jacking off, hit him in the stomach while he was jacking off, and basically, it was on a daily basis.

Q. Did she mention strangulation?

A Yes.

Q. Did she say 'defccate in the mouth"?

A. Yes.

Q. The defendant was present when she was asked that question?

A. Yes, he was.

Q. Did you ever have any conversations with Farah where she voiced to you that she was afraid of the defendant?

A. On numerous occasions.

Beeler said he moved to Victoria, Texas, in July 1994 to start his law practice there, and that Farah Fratta had hired another lawyer in Houston.

The next witness was the Houston attorney employed by Farah Fratta after Beeler's departure.

The new lawyer testified that the final custody trial had been preferentially set for October or November of 1994. The judge in the case had appointed Dr. Lawrence Abrams, a clinical psychologist, to make a psychological evaluation of both Farah and Bob Fratta and their three children to determine who best should be the guardian of the children, and make a recommendation based on his findings.

About the end of September or early October 1994, Farah's attorney had been notified by the psychologist that his evaluation of the family had been completed. (The psychologist usually contacts the attorneys on both sides and indicates what his recommendation will be, based on his study.)

The attorney said that usually the conclusions drawn in such a case would be given a great deal of weight by the judge because he appointed the professional who made them.

Farah's attorney reportedly had told her that she was going to get custody of the children because of what Dr. Abrams had decided.

Undoubtedly Fratta had heard about the evaluation results from his lawyer also. The verbal psychological evaluation report to the lawyers had been made about a month to a month and one half before the custody trial set for November 28, 1994. Farah Fratta was murdered on November 9, 1994.

The state now had Fratta's motives for murder before the jury: the possibility of big insurance money, dissatisfaction with his marital sex life, anger over his estranged wife's public disclosure of Fratta's perverted and disgusting sexual preferences and de-

mands, and the expected recommendation by Abrams
that the wife be given custody.

The courtroom was still as the slender boy walked
to the witness chair and sat down. Nine-year-old
Bradley Fratta bore a noticeable resemblance to the
man sitting at the counsel table. The youngster's eyes
stopped on his dad, then quickly moved away.

Siegler regretted having to call the solemn-faced
son of the victim to give testimony against his father,
although the boy probably did not realize that what
he said would be all that incriminating. But Siegler
knew the boy's story was key evidence. It would
show that his dad was paged and also was making
phone calls on the evening they went out to eat and
then to church for the catechism class—the evening
that his mom had died when a bad man shot her.

Gently and encouragingly, and with a quick smile,
Siegler brought the boy through the testimony before
the crowded courtroom, throwing in little unimportant
asides to get him relaxed and at ease. She covered
the events of that night, and he answered as he had
for the detectives during the investigation.

Defense Attorney Ackerman told Bradley that "I'm
your daddy's lawyer."

Bradley smiled, and waved at his father. Fratta
barely acknowledged the gesture by lifting one finger
and waving.

Q. You guys spent a lot of time with your daddy
after he moved out, didn't you?
A. Yes.

Q. Went a lot of places with him, like the zoo and Astroworld and Waterworld and stuff like that?

A. Yes.

Q. One thing about Daddy was that he was always making a lot of phone calls, wasn't he?

A. Yes.

Q. Got paged a lot, was on the phone a lot?

A. Uh, huh.

When the stoic youngster stepped down, several jurors and spectators rubbed tears from their eyes.

Siegler had achieved her purpose with the young witness. Bob Fratta making several phone calls and getting paged during the vital time period in which the murder happened was in the record from the most innocent of witnesses.

The brave little guy had come through for his mom, whether he was cognizant of that or not. And he didn't know his testimony had zapped his dad.

TWENTY-THREE

Presumably the last person to see and talk to Farah Fratta before she was ambushed by a waiting killer was Marribelle Gonzalez, her hairstylist and friend for about five years.

Gonzalez cut Farah Fratta's hair and also her children's.

Gonzalez would never forget their last visit. From the witness stand she told Prosecutor Casey O'Brien that the young mother came into the hair salon about 7:25 or 7:30 P.M. on Wednesday, November 9, 1994.

"She had a 7 o'clock appointment, but she came in late," the hairstylist testified. "She just needed a quick trim. She came in, she apologized, said she had to get some cash because she had written her last check.

"I shampooed her hair, and I brought her up to the front, and I trimmed around the side and the top and that was all. There was no blow dryer or anything. She left about 7:45 or 7:50. She was in a hurry. Something about she needed to be home by 8 o'clock because the kids were going to be home. She was wearing her workout outfit, workout clothes. She had just come from the gym."

O'Brien asked, "Was that typical of her?"

"Yes, she's done that before," Gonzalez said. "She was wearing, I think, they were black biker shorts with a leotard type thing and tennis shoes. When she left, she had wet hair, yes."

"Obviously, you never saw her again?" asked the assistant D.A.

"No, I didn't." There was a catch in her voice.

"Did you talk to her about her divorce or anything?"

The defense objected to the question on grounds of hearsay, and the objection was sustained by the judge.

O'Brien took another direction. "Was there a frequent conversation with her when you cut her hair? You cut her hair about five years. Was there an apex, was that [the divorce] pretty much the conversation, what all the conversation was about toward the end?"

Gonzales shrugged. "We just talked about, you know, what was going on."

When Farah drove away from the shop, she had no idea, of course, it was her last visit. Hardly ten minutes later, two bullets would rip through her newly trimmed hair, one slug lodging in her brain.

From Fratta and Prystash, the shooter knew her schedule well, and that she always kept it. Her father had trained her to be prompt and on time.

Another state witness, Rita St. Onge, an orthopedic nurse, was one of Farah Fratta's best friends. They usually talked on the phone several times a day. Their last conversation had been on the day before her death, St. Onge said sadly.

The nurse said Farah was "a close friend to me." They had met five years earlier at the President and

First Lady, where they both worked out. St. Onge also knew Bob Fratta, had met him at the gym. She told Prosecutor O'Brien that they all became friends, within a month probably.

"Can you describe Farah Fratta?" O'Brien asked.

"She was probably the most kind-hearted, nicest [person] I ever knew, a great mother."

"Did there come a time when it was apparent to you that there were problems with Farah and Bob?"

"Yes."

"Did he ever tell you anything specifically about what he desired out of their marriage?"

"Yes."

"What did he tell you?"

"He was bored sexually and he wanted an open marriage, and he wanted her to sleep with other women in front of him."

O'Brien asked, "When Bob Fratta talked to you about wanting an open marriage, did he say to you what open marriage meant to him?"

"To be able to have sex with other people. He was bored."

"Based on all you saw surrounding the marriage between the defendant and Farah Fratta, how would you characterize Farah's attempts to keep the marriage together?"

"She wanted a normal marriage. She wanted it to work."

"Did Bob Fratta ever come on to you?"

"Yes. He tried to kiss me at the doctor's office where I worked. He asked me to kiss him." She refused and never told Farah because she didn't want to further complicate her friend's marriage.

"How would you describe Bob Fratta?"

"I thought he was weird. I thought he had an unusual sex drive, and I really don't know what he was looking for."

St. Onge said she had talked to Farah the last time on the day before her death.

"Did Farah Fratta ever say anything to you in those phone conversations regarding her feelings about Bob Fratta?"

"Yes."

"Without telling us what she told you, describe her state of mind based on what you heard."

"She was extremely scared."

A longtime coworker and friend of Farah Fratta, Kitty Waters, described the separation and divorce-custody fight as "a very emotional breakup for both of them."

She said she last talked to Farah on the afternoon of the day she was killed, Wednesday.

"She was afraid. She was very subdued."

"How do you know she was afraid?" O'Brien asked the witness.

"Not from what she said, but how she said it. Her voice got very low. Her voice always got very low when something was disturbing her. When she was very emotional."

O'Brien asked, "Was the conversation you were having at that time when you noticed her being depressed and terrified about Bob Fratta?"

"Yes, sir."

Those who knew her best had been aware for some time that Farah Fratta was in fear for her life from her wrathful husband, especially since giving the deposition that publicly disclosed his sickening sexual appetites and demands.

* * *

Crescentia McAllister, a social worker who had made an investigation of Bob Fratta, was a little shaken when she interviewed him at his home.

Speaking of his boa python "pet," she said, "I asked him would he cover the pet up."

Equally startling to her were some of Fratta's comments.

"Did Bob Fratta ever say anything to you regarding what he was afraid Farah might have told you about him?" O'Brien asked.

"He mentioned she may have mentioned about adultery or that he was a flirt."

"And did he give you an explanation for that?"

"He denied the allegation. He said that he flirted on occasion, and it was for self-gratification."

"Did he say anything to you regarding his desire for an open marriage?

"He said he offered that to the mother to try and keep the family together. That he wanted to continue to be an active father with the children and his reason for asking that was he also wanted to have an affair, they live together and maybe even include the mother in the relationship."

"What kind of relationship?"

"Sexual relationship."

"Between who?"

"Himself and another female and the mother."

"For a three-way relationship—Bob Fratta, Farah Fratta and another woman?"

"Yes."

The murder trial was moving along. The testimony of Daren and Laura Hoelscher and Elizabeth Campbell who had heard and witnessed portions of the gunshot death of their neighbor, Farah Fratta, held the jury spellbound. Daren Hoelscher's description of his efforts to help the mortally wounded woman and his gripping recollection of administering last rites to the obviously dying victim were a dramatic account.

Laura Hoelscher was still affected by the nightmarish happenings viewed through the front windows of their home on November 9, 1994. The graphic testimony by the Hoelschers and Campbell obviously moved the ten men and two women on the jury.

TWENTY-FOUR

Tension was high among those who knew her role in the Farah Fratta murder case when attractive Mary Gipp took the witness chair.

Here was the woman who knew in advance that Farah Fratta would be murdered, knew who would do it and exactly when. Knew it a week or more before the hit.

But she had not warned the potential victim or notified the police.

Casey O'Brien, as requested by Siegler, would do the questioning of the witness who was a key part of their case, yet who would undoubtedly come across to the jury as someone who could have prevented the taking of a life and did not do it. O'Brien knew his job was to get her testimony before the jury so that, though the jurors might dislike her personally, they still would believe what she had to say.

She said she first met Joe Prystash in January 1993 at the President and First Lady gym. She said she had known Bob Fratta as "Bob" for four years, but had never known his last name.

She testified that Prystash and Fratta met frequently or talked on the phone "every day the last few weeks prior to Farah's death."

O'Brien asked her to tell the jury about a statement she had made to another member of the President and First Lady Spa, Mike Edens, a week or so before November 9, 1994.

She related that Prystash and Fratta had gone into the locker room at the gymnasium to talk. Whenever Prystash told her he was "going to talk to Bob," she knew what that meant. They were talking about the murder of Farah Fratta.

She testified that she "was scared" and "had an unbelievable feeling that I couldn't believe, that they were going to, that they were planning this murder."

She related that while talking to Edens, she told him that "Bob wanted to have Farah killed and he wanted Joe to kill Farah."

O'Brien asked, "And you were angry and shocked, is that what you are telling us?"

"Yes."

In her testimony she said Prystash and Howard Guidry, who lived next door, left together the evening of the murder. Both were wearing black clothing. They were in Prystash's silver, four-door Nissan with only one working headlight. She knew what they were going to do.

Gipp said she had left work early because she could not concentrate.

Three days before the killing she also had left early, intending to call Farah Fratta and warn her. But she could not find her address book with Farah's name in it, she said.

And she did not know Farah's husband's last name, as she mentioned earlier.

"Did you ever call?"

"No."

O'Brien asked her, "Could you have called the

gym? Couldn't you have called the President and First Lady?"

"I could have." No explanation was forthcoming.

"What were you going to tell Farah?"

"I was going to tell her that Bob was going to have her killed."

"Did you ever call her?"

"No."

"Why?"

"I don't know. I just didn't."

"Were you in love with Joe Prystash?"

"Yes."

Gipp went on to describe the events of that November 9 evening—Prystash and Guidry coming back, Prystash going into the bedroom and unloading the gun, throwing two shells in the garbage, then hiding the gun. Told of her retrieving and saving the shells and of writing down information from the gun on a slip of paper.

"Let me show you State's Exhibit No. 60, Mary." O'Brien extended the .38-caliber Police Bulldog Special toward her, saying, "It's unloaded, okay. You want to look at that a second? I'll hold it. Do you recognize it?"

"Yes."

"Is that the gun you saw Joe unload?"

"Yes."

Referring to when Gipp watched Prystash unloading the gun, O'Brien asked, "Did you say anything to him, Mary?"

"I asked him if he, if they, had killed her?"

"What did he say?"

"He said yes. I asked him if she was dead, if he

knew that she was dead, and he said, 'Yes.' I said, 'How do you know?' and he said he saw her. He said that Howard killed her in the garage."

"And when did he see her, did he say?"

"He just said he saw her, and walked out."

She said Prystash left, saying he was going to the gym to meet Bob.

"What was he going to get at the gym?"

"He was going to get a thousand dollars from Bob."

"Hey! Listen to my question!" O'Brien said sharply. "I asked you *what* he was going to get."

"Money."

"Thank you, I didn't mean to snap at you. About what time was it he left?"

"Before nine p.m. I think."

Gipp said when Prystash was gone, she took the information from the gun, writing it on a slip of paper.

"Mary, let me show what has been marked as State's Exhibit 58. Do you recognize this? Is this what you wrote down?"

"Yes."

"Read that, please."

Gipp took the paper, then read: "Police Bulldog .38 Special, Charter Arms Corp., Stratford, Conn., 77150."

"Did you write down a serial number?"

"I guess it's 77191590."

"Why did you write this stuff down, Mary?"

"Because I knew what they had done was wrong, and I knew they [police] would need it later."

She later, after being subpoenaed to the grand jury, turned over the piece of paper to her lawyer and a detective, she testified.

Gipp testified she had been given immunity from prosecution on a charge of tampering with evidence if she would testify about what she knew.

"In other words, you were made to testify, weren't you?"

"Yes."

After that, said Gipp, detectives hooked a tape recorder to her phone, with instructions to record any of Bob Fratta's phone calls. She did record one, but there was nothing pertinent to the investigation.

Gipp testified that Prystash told her the next morning that Howard Guidry had waited in the garage and shot Farah two times in the head, that Howard called him where Prystash was waiting at a pay phone in front of Food City supermarket and that he picked him up. She said Howard called on her cell phone.

That morning after the killing, when they heard on the news that witnesses saw a one-headlight car, Prystash replaced the broken headlight on the Nissan.

"In addition to the one thousand dollars you said he was going to get, did Prystash ever tell you anything else he was going to receive for the murder of Farah Fratta?"

"A Jeep."

"Pass the witness."

Defense Attorney John Ackerman had a theory of his own that he was going to put before the jury during his cross-examination of the witness.

Ackerman picked up the same gun identified earlier by Gipp, and said, "Miss Gipp, I want to show you this so you will understand I'm talking about this particular weapon when I discuss it with you, okay?"

"Yes, sir." Mary Gipp had no idea what tack Fratta's lawyer would take, but she was not expecting an easy time ahead.

Ackerman sat down at the table again before he spoke. "Now Joe Prystash had that particular gun in his possession back as early as June 1994, did he not?"

"Yes, I believe so."

"Five months or more prior to November 9 when Farah Fratta was killed?"

"Yes."

"And he told you he had gotten it from Bob Fratta, did he not?"

"Correct."

"And he told you that it was payment for some work he had done on Bob Fratta's car, didn't he?"

"I'm not sure."

"He told you later he wasn't going to give it back to Bob Fratta, didn't he?"

"Yes."

"There was indication that Mr. Fratta had asked for it back, and Joe said he wasn't going to give it back, correct?"

"No, he just made a statement that he wasn't going to give it back."

"Did you ever hear of a person named William Planter?"

"Yes."

Anybody who read the Houston newspaper or watched the local TV news had heard of Planter. He was a former peace officer who had been arrested after contacting Lex Baquer with an offer to kill Bob Fratta.

Baquer had notified detectives, who set up a trap for the would-be hired killer. Planter had been charged with attempting to set up a murder and later was found guilty and sentenced to nineteen years in prison.

"Did you know that Joe Prystash was in some way associated with William Planter?"

"Yes."

"In fact, Joe Prystash told you that William Planter was a hit man, did he not?"

"Yes."

"That he would arrange to have people killed?"

"Yes."

"And there was a time when you even believed Joe was working for him?"

"Yes."

"And you continued to let Joe Prystash live in your house?"

"That's correct."

"And continued to share your bed with him?"

"That's correct."

"You told this jury today that when you were at President and First Lady on a particular night and had a conversation with Mike Edens, you were 'shocked and angry' were your words, correct?"

"Yes."

"And you also told the jury you had been hearing about this for quite a long period of time, correct? You knew about it before you ever went there [the gym] that night, according to your testimony, and your testimony is that Mr. Prystash told you about that much earlier, isn't that what you're telling the jury?"

"Yes."

"You knew, according to what you told the jury,

that there were daily conversations between Bob Fratta and Joe Prystash? For weeks?"

"That's correct."

"So you stayed shocked and angry for weeks, right?"

"Yes, sir."

"This incident at the President and First Lady that you describe today as being shocking and producing anger wasn't any different at that point than it had been for weeks prior to that, right?"

"I can't imagine you asked me that, but yes, sir."

"So you stayed shocked and angry for weeks. But you didn't call the police?"

"No, sir, I didn't. I made a mistake."

"You didn't call Farah Fratta? You didn't call anybody?"

"No, I didn't."

"And you continued to let Joe Prystash live in your house, and you continued to share your bed with him?

"Yes, I did."

"And you're still shocked and angry, I presume?"

"No, I'm scared."

"You told us you've known Bob Fratta about four years?"

"Yes, maybe a little more."

"And you spoke to Bob Fratta at times?"

"Probably."

"You knew his name was Bob Fratta?"

"No, I didn't know what his last name was. I never knew his last name."

"What kind of a car were you driving on November 9, 1994?

"An Acclaim."

"And that's the car you said the cellular phone was in?"

"Correct."

"It's kind of a bad neighborhood you live in, isn't it?"

"No, I don't think so."

"High crime neighborhood?"

"No, it's very low actually."

"After November 9, 1994, nearly four months went by before you gave a statement to police on March 4, 1995, correct?"

"Correct."

"And during that four-month period I take it you remained shocked and angered?"

"No, sir."

"So you got over that?"

"I'm still not over it."

"Knowing Farah Fratta was dead caused you to somehow get over being shocked and angry. You didn't stay shocked and angry?"

"I'm still angry."

"You stayed angry through that whole four-month period?"

"Angry about what? What is your question?"

"Well, those were your words. You said you were shocked and angry about Bob Fratta and Joe Prystash meeting at the President and First Lady on a particular day that you talked to Mike Edens. Then you told me you were shocked and angry for the six months prior to the murder, and now you told me you were shocked and angry for the four months after that. Those were your words. I just want to know if you just stayed shocked and angry every day after November 9, 1994 until you gave your statement to police on March 4, 1995?"

"Perhaps."

"And during the time you were shocked and angry you continued to live with Joe Prystash?"

"Yes, I did."

"And continued to share your bed with Joe Prystash?"

"Actually, we broke up right after that. We had a lot of problems right after that."

"After Joe Prystash was arrested and placed in jail, you went there to visit him frequently?"

"Yes, I still do."

"Thank you. You intended to marry him, did you not?"

"I love Joe. I'm sorry. I love him. No, I would not marry him."

"Were you making plans to marry him while he was still in jail?"

"No."

"Never discussed that with anybody?"

"About marrying him? Yes, I discussed it."

"While he was in jail?"

"Yes."

"Your Honor, I have no further questions," Ackerman said.

Mary Gipp's ordeal in the witness chair was over. It would be up to the jury what to make of her testimony.

Prosecutor Kelly Siegler said later in an interview, "Though she could have prevented all this, she did finally tell the truth about everything she knew. I do believe that. I don't believe in the end she tried to hide anything about Joe or Howard or Bob. I think she just got attracted to the wrong man when she got attracted to Joe. She liked that edge of danger or whatever it was she saw in him. Lost sight of her senses. Really wanted to be loved. And didn't use her normal judgment. I don't think she's a *bad* person. I just think she made a stupid decision."

TWENTY-FIVE

The gun taken from Howard Guidry after the Klein State Bank robbery had been identified by Mary Gipp as the same weapon Joe Prystash unloaded in their apartment on the murder night. The serial number jotted down by Gipp matched the one on the gun. Detective Ronnie Roberts through the Alcohol, Tobacco and Firearms federal agency had determined the gun was purchased by Bob Fratta in 1982.

Next, the state would show that the gun had fired the shot that killed Farah Fratta. Charlie Anderson, chief firearms examiner for the Houston Police Department Firearms Laboratory, had made the ballistics test.

The bullet that had been removed at the crime-scene from the child's toy life preserver on the garage wall and another slug recovered from the victim's brain were examined by Anderson under a comparison microscope. They were compared with bullets test fired from the .38-caliber Police Bulldog Special revolver used by Guidry in the killing and the bank robbery.

Explaining his testing procedures, Anderson said, "I tried to determine the condition of the weapon. I checked it to see if it was capable of discharging a cartridge and it was. It was in very good condition. There were two bullets and some fragments to be examined to determine if they were fired in that particular weapon."

Casey O'Brien asked: "Were you able or did you determine the bullets couldn't be eliminated as having been fired from State's Exhibit 60 [the recovered weapon]? Were you able to determine whether either or both were fired from that gun?"

"I was able to determine that one of them was fired from that particular weapon. The other I was not; I could not positively identify it. However, I could not eliminate it."

"Which one, sir, can you tell us which one you were able to positively identify as having been fired from State Exhibit 60?"

"Exhibit No. 49, which is the one recovered from the life jacket [on the garage wall]."

"Based on your opinion, No. 49 was fired from No. 60?"

"That's correct."

"Any question in your mind?"

"No, sir."

There were not sufficient characteristics on the other bullet, or fragment, for him to determine positively that it was fired from the weapon. The damage he found on the slug prevented making a definite identification. But he said the slug did have "a lot of individual characteristics that were the same as that firearm. But not enough to make a positive identification."

The bullet bad been damaged apparently by hitting bone.

* * *

Bob Fratta had no timidity about his bizarre sexual preferences or his extensive search for a killer to murder his wife. He practically had shouted this information from the roof tops.

That became apparent as the prosecutors paraded a string of both female and male witnesses who gave shocking and sickening testimony about Fratta's revolting sexual likes that finally led Farah Fratta to seek a divorce and custody of their children.

Minnie Lawrence told the jury of going from telephone sex with Fratta to his favorite sexual activity of her sitting and defecating on his face; she led the revolting testimony. The weighty desktop publisher said that Fratta preferred fat women.

Lawrence had been the only one of all those people whom Fratta approached trying to find a killer to "do" his wife who had contacted the sheriff's department in spite of the embarrassing story she had to tell.

The college student Penny Adams related the experiences with Fratta that happened after first meeting him in the company of a transvestite and a gay in the Montrose section of Houston.

She recalled his persistent efforts to get her and her friend to change their clothes in front of him, then pursuing her with strange sexual requests until she finally broke off with him.

There were the string of bodybuilder pals from the President and First Lady gym who testified how Fratta had kept after them to kill his wife or find someone who would. They all testified that hey thought he was joking and did not take his actions seriously.

There were his former fellow public safety officers at Missouri City, who remembered not only Fratta's efforts to hire a killer, but also his favorite sexual activity of having women defecate and urinate in his face. His sexual tastes were known throughout the fire stations where he worked.

There were witnesses who told the jury of his wanting an open marriage where he could have sex with other women, with other women and his wife together or maybe another man thrown in. Or a three-way tryst with his wife, him and a male homosexual or a lesbian, or his wife with a lesbian or a transvestite.

The lurid, repulsive testimony left some of the spectators ill and almost ready to abandon the sensational trial.

There was Christine Raisaman, the X-ray technologist, who told of Fratta's rude and demanding call to the trauma-emergency room of Hermann Hospital wanting to know if his wife was dead or alive and saying he wanted to bring the children to see her before she died.

And the testimony of Karry Lennon, the insurance claims clerk, whom Fratta called to ask when the life insurance policy on his wife would be paid, thinking that he was the beneficiary. The call had come only two days after her slaying.

Two women from the church where Fratta took his three children on the murder night took the stand to tell of his actions at the church. Of most interest from an evidence standpoint were the numerous phone calls he kept leaving to make on the office phone, and the several calls to his pager.

The detectives of the sheriff department's homicide unit detailed their extensive investigation from the night of the murder and over the next few months, countless hours of running out leads and interviewing witnesses and possible suspects.

The state rested its case after the testimony of insurance claims clerk Lennon.

Judge Burdette said to Defense Attorney Charlton: "The state having announced they have rested, what says the defense, sir?"

"We are ready to proceed," Charlton said. "However, we at this time move for an instructed verdict of not guilty for the failure of the state to prove that Mr. Fratta engaged in the conduct that he hired anybody to do anything. There's been no proof of that, and certainly, more than enough proof I suppose to get to the jury on the issue of Mr. Prystash and Mr. Guidry, but no proof that Mr. Fratta hired them, and so we respectfully move for a directed verdict on that basis."

"Your motion for an instructed verdict is denied," the judge said.

The defense called as its first witness Dr. Edward Freidman who, in addition to private practice as a psychologist, was employed by the Harris County Mental Health and Mental Retardation in the Adult Forensic Service division.

Questioned by Attorney Charlton, Freidman testified about various tests he had administered to Fratta and the results. He said he initially spent about four hours interviewing Fratta and two hours giving him ink blot tests and "other projective tests."

Charlton asked, "At my request did you specifically conduct an evaluation in the area known as sexual deviancy?"

Freidman said that that was the reason for administering the Rorschach ink-blot test.

Asked by the lawyer to explain how a patient's reactions to ink blots enable trained experts to detect psychological disorders, the doctor said, "It's a little bit like looking at clouds. A cloud is really just a cloud, but when you look at a cloud, if you watch it for a while, you can see different things. And different people or even the same person at active times will see different things in the same cloud.

"Ink blots are similar to that."

He further explained, "All they really are are designs made with ink on pieces of paper and then printed on pieces of cardboard.

"When people are asked to look at them and describe what they see, or what it is it reminds them of, or what they think it could be, what they see is determined by their own personality or their own needs or their own moods.

"And since the same ink blots have been used over and over again for about seventy-five years, and a great deal of information has been gathered how people with similar kinds of personalities and similar kinds of psychopathology or psychological disturbances perceive the same ink blots, it enables us to say things about an individual's personality and about their psychological and emotional functioning based upon what they see when they look at these cards."

Charlton displayed several ink blots and asked how Fratta had reacted to each of them.

The answers from the psychologist ranged from "insect, butterfly, a bat or perhaps a bird" to "two people doing something," or, turning it upside down, "a child's top" to "two women who were bending over picking up bowling ball bags" to "a fur pelt or fur rug" to "two little Indian girls" to a "bouquet of flowers."

Charlton asked, "Now, as a preliminary matter based on all the testing you conducted of Robert Alan Fratta, did you find any evidence of psychopathology?"

"No, I really didn't."

Now came the nitty gritty.

"Let's specifically discuss practices known as defecation, urination and the sexual relationship context," Charlton said. "Those kind of practices go by the specific name of paraphilia, do they not?"

"Yes."

"Let me back up a minute. what is meant by the term 'psychopathology'?"

"It means a personality disturbance significant enough to affect a person's functioning in one or more areas of their life. You know, negatively."

Charlton asked Freidman to describe what is meant by "the paraphilia such as defecation and urination?"

The doctor paused. "Well, they are, I don't recall a specific and exact definition, but basically what it comes down to they are ways of obtaining sexual arousal and sexual gratification by, you know, avenues other than—what at least to our society—are basically considered normal ways of becoming sexually aroused and obtaining sexual gratification."

"Based on the types of tests that you conducted, did you see any evidence that Mr. Fratta suffered from paraphilia that we discussed?"

"No, I did not."

"Why would those ink blots tell you that?' asked Charlton.

"Because again, at least, the very least in our society, these paraphilias, these what in our culture are deviant ways of obtaining sexual gratification, do present significant conflicts for an individual, and usually, not usually, I think always, indicates some kind of disturbance in the sexual part of a person's personality. And when that occurs, when there is some kind of disturbance in the person's sexual development, it's usually seen in psychological tests such as the ink blot test."

Continuing, as one or two jurors began scratching their heads or sighing, Freidman said:

"Because a person, because conflicts—the kind of conflicts that occur around sexual practices or sexual needs, such as these deviant sexual practices and needs—cause a person to see different things in ink blots from somebody who obtains sexual arousal and gratification in the more usual, what we refer to, as in the normal way."

Charlton asked, "Why would an individual who would enjoy that kind of thing or do it on a frequent basis find manifest conflicts?"

"Because in our culture that is so unusual and it's considered deviant and is a basis for feeling guilty, shame, emotions such as that."

TWENTY-SIX

Kelly Siegler had spent long hours poring over psychology books, talking to psychologists and psychiatrists, and meeting at length with the highly respected Dr. Greg Redi, who was in charge of evaluating applicants for the Houston Police Department.

She had obtained paperwork filled out in 1984 when one particular applicant, Bob Fratta, was reviewed and rejected by Dr. Redi. She had read books and scholarly magazines and scientific reports on aberrant psychological behavior, to the point, she said, that she was beginning to feel a little dippy herself.

Now, as she stared directly at him, she bluntly asked the psychologist for the defense, "Dr. Freidman, do you ever get told by lay people or non-psychology people that this is a bunch of bull?" She could have made it stronger.

The doctor said, "Yes, sometimes."

"Sometimes. Could you tell the jury who Dr. Lois Freidman is?"

"My wife, also a psychologist, yes."

"Also subpoenaed to perhaps testify in this case?"

"I believe so, yes."

"And you and your wife have discussed the fact that she interviewed this defendant back in 1984, is that correct?"

"She told me she interviewed him, but we could not discuss it."

"Okay, because she couldn't talk about it with you because it's confidential information, as far as the Houston Police Department is concerned?"

"Yes."

"But you are aware that your wife interviewed this defendant in the course of his applying for a job with the Houston Police Department?"

"Yes, I am."

"Did you know, Dr. Freidman, that your wife showed this defendant those very same ink blot tests so many years ago?"

"No, I did not."

"Let's talk about the ink blot test for a minute. It's my understanding after talking to your wife that some of the key words you all look for when you show people those pictures are words like 'torn,' 'tear' and things like that, is that right?"

"That depends on when you say key words. It depends on what you're looking for a key to."

"Okay, well let's just say generally speaking, if someone mentions the word 'torn' or 'tear' or something like that in the course of looking at all these little pictures, doesn't that say something to you as a psychologist?"

"Yes, it does."

"What does it say, Doctor?"

"It really depends on the context of it. It depends on specifically what is being, what the individual has said, and also it depends on the context in which it is said. It could mean different things."

"Okay, let's just talk about these then. Did you ever get a chance to review the notes your wife made when she interviewed this defendant years ago?"

"No."

"Let me hand these back to you, sir, and let's start with the first one."

At this point, a break was taken in the proceedings.

Siegler resumed her questioning later. "Dr. Freidman, I think I was asking you about the sentence completion test when we took our break. Is that correct: that test is one where you give someone a word and then there's a blank there, and they are asked to complete the sentence?"

"Yes."

"If the word given was 'a man' and then a blank, they could fill in whatever they wanted to in that blank after the word 'man'?"

"That's correct."

"They could put anything such as 'man is the stronger sex,' the 'man earned a living,' 'men make good daddies,' but if the answer was 'men don't turn me on,' that's kind of unusual wouldn't you agree with me, Doctor?"

"It's unusual."

" 'Men don't turn me on' is unusual?"

"I just said it was unusual."

"And if this defendant said that back in 1984, that would say a little bit about him wouldn't it, sir?"

"I'm not sure what it would say."

"Sure would say something though, wouldn't it?"

"I said it was unusual. I agree."

"Would you agree with me, Dr. Freidman . . . Let me start like this: When you first met Bob Fratta, who introduced you to him?"

"Mr. Charlton."

"His lawyer representing him for capital murder introduced you to Bob Fratta?"

"That's correct."

"When you administered these tests to him like the ink blot tests did anybody go with you?"

"No."

"Just went by yourself?"

"Certainly."

"Would you agree with me that any test administered to anybody you would get a fairer reading, or a fairer answer, from someone when they didn't know what they were being tested for as opposed to if they knew what they were being tested for?"

"I really don't understand your question."

"Okay, let's say it again. When you were introduced to this defendant by his lawyer, Mike Charlton, Mr. Fratta knows that he's going to stand trial for capital murder, right?"

"Yes, correct."

"Which do you think would get fairer answers, back when he answered the ink blot test in 1984 as compared to when he answered these ink blot tests to the psychologist introduced to him by the lawyer who represents him for capital murder?"

Freidman said that when he gave the tests to Fratta "there were indications that he answered in a very open and honest way. I can't speak to how he did or didn't do eleven or twelve years ago."

"But your wife is a qualified psychologist, isn't she, Dr. Freidman?"

"Yes, she is."

"I think I added up the sum total of time you spent with this man. About eight hours, is that correct?"

"It was more around ten hours."

"And in part of your evaluation of this defendant you were asked to determine if he had any type of sexual deviant personality?"

"Yes."

"Did you ever say, 'Bob Fratta, do you have a sexual deviant personality?' Did you ever ask him that question?"

"No, I did not."

"Did you ever ask him what type of sex he preferred? Did you ever ask him that question?"

"Not directly, no. We discussed it during the interview, however, and he indicated to me nothing about preferring what we refer to as deviant sex."

"I guess I wouldn't have brought it up either if nobody asked me. Did you ever ask him, 'Do you like deviant sexual behavior?' "

"No."

"Did you ever talk to Dr. Larry Abrams?"

"I have spoken to Dr. Abrams about Mr. Fratta."

"Are you aware that Dr. Abrams evaluated this defendant?"

"Yes."

"Are you aware that this defendant admitted to Dr. Larry Abrams that he did—"

The defense objected that question assumed facts not in evidence and the objection was sustained by the judge.

Siegler continued.

"So whether or not this defendant made any admissions or not to Dr. Abrams, you don't know because you never picked up the phone and asked him, did you, sir?"

"That's correct."

"Did you ever talk to Minnie Lawrence?"

"No."

"Did you ever see Minnie Lawrence's witness statement?"

"No."

"Have you ever been told anything about the way she testified here in court last week?"

"No, I have not."

"Have you any idea of what Minnie Lawrence told this jury as far as this defendant's sexual preference, do you, sir?"

"I think I've answered I don't know anything about Minnie Lawrence."

"Have you ever talked to any of the firemen or policemen this defendant worked with during his shift at the Missouri City Police Department [Public Safety Department]?"

"No."

"Did you ever ask this defendant specifically what he liked to do in sex?"

"As I was saying before, Mr. Fratta discussed sexual activity with me."

"Did you ever ask Bob Fratta if he liked to have his female partners defecate in his mouth?"

"No."

"Did you ever ask Bob Fratta if he liked to have his wife, his wife, Farah, defecate in his mouth?"

"No."

"Did you ever ask Bob Fratta if he used to follow her around the kitchen in the morning when she got up, sniffing at her rear end and waiting for her to go to the bathroom? Did you ever ask him that?"

"No."

"Did you ever ask him whether or not he used to get her to eat food the minute she got home from work so she could poop in his mouth?"

"No."

"Did you ever ask Bob Fratta if he liked to have her urinate on his face?"

"No."

"Did you ever ask Bob Fratta if he liked to lick [women]? Did you ever ask him that?"

"No."

"If he told you that he did, if he would have answered any of those questions yes, would that change your mind as to whether he's got a sexual deviant personality?"

"I can't answer that question yes or no, Ms. Siegler."

"You are telling me that if he had told you that he liked it when his wife pooped in his mouth so he could eat it, you can't tell me yes, that means he's got a sexual deviant personality problem?"

"If he had told me that, yes, I would have, that would have told me something."

"That was my question: If he had told you that, if you would have asked him that, that would have told you something?"

"I didn't have to ask him because he discussed without my asking him what his sexual preferences were and were not.

"Since I . . . since he had already answered these

questions without me asking him. I didn't have to ask him these things. I didn't feel I had to."

"Did you ever ask him about his friend, Peaches, a transvestite?"

"No."

"Dr. Freidman, did you ever ask Bob Fratta if his wife beat on him, slapped and kicked him when he ejaculated?"

"No, I didn't."

"Is it your testimony to this jury that you had a completely thorough and open and honest conversation with this defendant about his sexual preferences?"

"I feel that I did."

"And if he had engaged in any of these things I have just described to you and told you that he had, if you would have asked him, it would have said to you that he had a sexual deviant personality problem?"

"I did ask him—can you repeat the question?"

"If Mr. Fratta told you that he did like to do any of these things I just described to you, if you would have asked him, that it would have told you that he had a sexual deviant personality problem, wouldn't it have?"

"I have two questions there, and I can't—I don't know which one to answer."

"Okay, answer this one: If he would have told you, yes, he liked these things, would that have told you that he has a sexual problem?"

"Yes."

"You told this jury that you used to work at evaluating applicants for the Houston Police Department.

Isn't it true that your job lasted a great total of six months, sir?"

"I believe it was seven or eight months."

"Okay, and your boss at that time was Dr. Greg Redi, who still has that same job today?"

"Yes."

"And Dr. Redi fired you at the end of that seven- or eight-month period, didn't he, sir?"

"No, he did not."

"Well, he let you go, didn't he?"

"No, I resigned."

"You're saying you resigned?"

"I resigned."

TWENTY-SEVEN

The brain game testimony must have seemed endless to the jurors, with all of the convoluted questions and answers about the psychological side of accused murderer Bob Fratta.

Prosecutor Siegler, continuing her cross-examination of the witness, wanted to clarify some of the hundred-dollar words used in the business of psychology.

She said, "You define psychopathology as a personality disturbance enough to affect one or more areas of one's life?"

"That's correct."

"Is that the same thing, psychopathology, as someone who has an indication of being a psychopath?"

"No."

"What's the difference between the two?"

"The term psychopath has not been used for several decades. The term currently used is antisocial personality disorder. I can't give you the exact definition, but basically it's an individual who on a repeated basis engages in antisocial acts which violate the rights of other people, and you know, I think you know, without looking at the definition basically, you know as I said, I think we all are in agreement, as to what antisocial behavior is."

"I'm sorry, what did you just say?" Siegler asked.

"I think we are probably in agreement or understand what antisocial behavior is."

Siegler asked, "Do you agree with me that any of those sexual acts we talked about are those that violate the norm?"

"They violate norms, yes."

Freidman agreed that his testing showed signs of narcissism in Fratta, the term meaning "a person who has an inflated sense of their own worth."

"If any of these sexual things we've talked about are true, would that indicate Bob Fratta was masochistic?" Siegler asked.

"I would have to know more about specifics."

"Okay, I'll be specific for you, Dr. Freidman. If it were true that Bob Fratta liked to have women poop in his mouth so he could eat it, would that indicate that he's masochistic?"

"Yes."

"Would you agree with me, Dr. Freidman, that if any of the things we have discussed are true about Bob Fratta's preferences, it would obviously change an opinion about the man."

"Yes, it would."

She asked if Fratta had admitted the bizarre sexual practices, discussed previously with Dr. Larry Abrams, a court-appointed psychologist who interviewed him, that he had done those type things sexually would that change Freidman's opinion about Fratta?

"Are you talking about the things alleged in the deposition?"

"Yes, sir."

"Yes, it would."

Questioned by Siegler about the results of an MMPI test (Minnesota Multiphasic Personality Inventory) that he gave to Fratta, Freidman agreed that the defendant had scored high on the psychopathic deviant and the paranoia scales. He attributed this to Fratta's situation of being in jail at the time.

"Would you agree with me this Scale 4 psychopathic deviate is probably one of the most important scales you look at on the MMPI?"

"Yes."

Siegler asked Freidman if he would agree that the high scores by Fratta on psychological deviation and paranoia were in the range that only one person in a thousand would be classified.

"You're not going to disagree with me, are you?"

"No. I assume you are getting this having done some research or homework on it yourself."

"You wouldn't disagree with me would you when I say that prison inmates who score as high as Bob Fratta did on those scales would be immediately segregated if they tested that high?"

"No, I don't have the basis for either agreeing or disagreeing."

Siegler pointed out to Freidman that he never mentioned the MMPI test when testifying about his evaluation of Fratta until Siegler had asked him on cross-examination if he had ever done an MMPI test on the defendant.

Siegler then bore down on the poor scores Fratta made on the paranoia and the psychological deviation scales.

"After you gave Bob Fratta this MMPI test, and you got those original high scores, then you had a discussion with Mr. Charlton about the scores you got?"

"We had discussed the extent to which his score might be affected by his situation before I ever gave the test."

"But you are the one who decided why his scores were that high. You speculated, did you not, that the reason he scored so high was because he had been in jail so long?"

"That's correct."

"You decided that?"

"I'm a psychologist. That's what I do. I try to decide why people's psychological states are the way they are."

"And when you tried to understand why he scored so high, then you curved his grade?"

"No, I didn't change the grade, Ms. Siegler."

"In any event, you talked to Mr. Charlton about how high he scored on these scales. You went back, had a little talk with Bob Fratta in the jail and came up with these new answers?"

"I didn't change any answers or come up with any new answers. The original score is still there. That is still the score which he obtained. I merely did this to demonstrate."

"Why you thought he might have scored so high?"

"That's correct."

"And one more thing, back when your wife tested Bob Fratta in 1984, he was pretty high on that paranoia scale even back then, wasn't he?"

"Yes, he was."

* * *

Bob Fratta's association with gays, lesbians and transvestites came into the courtroom spotlight during one phase of Siegler's questioning of Dr. Freidman.

"On the last page of all your notes, did you see where Bob Fratta told you at times during separation from his wife he went to gay bars?"

"Yes."

"And he looked for a lesbian bar to indulge his fantasy of being with two women at one time?"

"Yes."

"And he told you that he went to a drag queen show, and he enjoyed the entertainment?"

"Yes."

"Periodically he returned there when he was lonely, although he denied homosexual activity at any time?"

"Correct. He liked the atmosphere of gay bars because he didn't have to worry about macho challenges like there were in country-and-western bars. Yes, that's what he notes."

"He also told you he knows one transvestite who will testify that they did have sex?"

"Yes."

Fratta himself had tried to explain all the times he had asked people if they would kill or find someone to murder his wife, according to Dr. Freidman's notes when he interviewed him.

Siegler asked, "He told you that he was so frustrated about his divorce that he joked about her death, hoping that she would hear about it and realize the extent of his frustration at her interference?"

"Yes."

"So all the times he talked to people about having his wife killed, he was just joking?"

"I don't know that. I only know what he told me at that time. What you just read."

The defense called Jay Newton, who was an attorney and employed as a physician's assistant to the doctor who had treated Farah Fratta during a period of stress and depression she suffered while engaged in the divorce-custody battle.

"At my request and our subpoena, did you bring with you the medical records of Farah Fratta?"

"Yes, I did."

"Now, how are those medical records you have in your hand, are they kept in—"

The prosecutors interrupted with a request to approach the bench for a conference with the judge. This is done out of the hearing of the jury when a controversial point needs to be hashed over by the lawyers.

Charlton told the judge that "these people treated Mrs. Fratta for a period of seven years. No time did she ever discuss with them, even while she was on a rigid regime of treatment for depression, at no time did she discuss the sexual deviance [of Bob Fratta]. The only time those came out were in the divorce action."

Kelly Siegler said, "Judge, this is a backdoor way of trying to get in she was on this antidepressant, and which in itself is not admissible. Because she didn't tell one person doesn't mean it didn't happen. It's irrevelant."

The judge permitted the testimony, with the name of the antidepressant excluded.

Charlton then asked the witness, "The kind of statements that people make, especially when they are made in the particular progress notes in this case, are they the kind of statements that normally doctors need to know about in order to make a certain prescription and certain diagnostic decision?"

"Yes, they are."

"Certain therapeutic decisions have to be made on the kinds of information that the patients would provide?"

"You base your diagnosis and treatment on all of the elements that the patients tell you."

"Now, I don't want you to discuss with me a specific medicine or brand name or anything like that, but in the course of the treatment of Farah was an antidepressant prescribed?"

"Yes."

"Based on your records, how long did the doctor treat Farah Fratta?"

"The first notes we have in our records are April 29, 1993, and the last visit was October 4, 1994."

"Now the principal complaints registered by Mrs. Fratta during this time period in question concerned the divorce, do they not?"

"The principal complaints were decreased energy, difficulty in sleeping and some general anxieties and concerns around a divorce."

"Based on the notes that the doctor took, or whoever took the notes at the time, Mrs. Fratta indicated she was under a lot of stress with court battles?"

"Yes, she did."

"Now I would like you to move down for a few lines [referring to the records], commence with the phrase, 'I'm fighting for full custody, not joint custody.' Is that correct?"

"That's correct."

Charlton also noted a complaint by Farah Fratta on the lack of aggressiveness of her then-attorney on her case, and other discussions about difficulty sleeping and nervousness and the notation that she was going to get another lawyer.

Other notes in the record mentioned her fear of losing her children, of the house perhaps going into foreclosure and the possibility of her children living with their dad.

"There're some allegations made against Mr. Fratta, are there not?"

"Yes, there are."

"She states in there specifically certain things Mr. Fratta did, one of which he prowls around her house at two A.M.?"

"That is stated."

TWENTY-EIGHT

Another witness was the thirty-three-year-old legal secretary, Marlene Anderson, who testified she had a normal romantic relationship with Bob Fratta when she dated him beginning in November 1993. She thought he was very nice and courteous and as normal as they come in their intimate relationship.

Never no nasty stuff.

She went to his house on a blind date, after being introduced to him by her friend, the pretty secretary testified.

"Did you enjoy Mr. Fratta's company?" the defense attorney asked.

"I did."

She said they "kind of dated, I guess, for about three months, and talked on the phone until probably May 1994."

She said that Fratta treated her extremely courteously, openly and honestly, and they later became sexually intimate.

"During your intimate relationship with Mr. Fratta did he ever suggest to you or attempt to manipulate you into acts of defecation or urination?"

"No, sir."

"Did he ever ask you to do any of these kind of acts in the closet?"

"No, sir."

She said when they eventually broke up, Fratta was open with her about it, and she was disappointed at their parting.

Under cross-examination, Anderson said they broke up because "he met somebody else."

"What was his attitude towards his wife?"

"I mean, it wasn't working. He was sorry about that. Just on the way he treated me, I would find it hard to believe that he murdered his wife, and I would still be seeing him, yes."

Arlene Tolbert, a freelance artist, recalled she met Fratta at random while standing in line at a Luby's Cafeteria.

She said they started talking casually and she liked him.

"I don't mean to ask a prying question, but I kind of have to," said Attorney Charlton. "Did your relationship with Bob evolve to the point where it became an intimate relationship?"

"Yes, sir."

"How long did the relationship last?"

"The whole relationship or the intimate?"

"The whole."

"Probably three to three and one half months."

"During that time the relationship was intimate?"

"Well, that's what I meant to say."

"Did Bob ever try to get you to engage in acts where he would have you defecate on him or urinate on him?"

"No, sir."

"Did he ever ask you to choke him while he masturbated?"

"Absolutely not."

"Ever ask you to participate in acts like this in a closet?"

"Absolutely not."

Richard Oaks, a lieutenant in the Missouri City Fire Department, had been Fratta's immediate supervisor for one and a half years. He described Fratta as a good firemen who "got along with people."

Defense Attorney Ackerman asked, "You no doubt heard about allegations that Robert Alan Fratta basically liked to have women defecate on him and urinate on him and acts of [a] similar nature. Did you ever hear that kind of talk around your fire station?"

"No, sir."

"If anybody in that fire station ever admitted to enjoy having people do those things, do you think you would have heard about it pretty quick?"

"Yes, sir, I would have."

On the matter of the $1,050 in cash found in the glove compartment in Fratta's car on the night of the murder, the defense called a witness who seemingly had an explanation for the money being there.

James Ray Thomas was asked by Defense Attorney Ackerman, "Were you aware that in late October or early November 1994 prior to the time that Farah Fratta was killed that Bob Fratta was having to replace the carpet in his home?"

"Yes, I was."

"You made arrangements for him, did you not, to get the padding for that carpet?"

"Yes, I did."

"And the cost for that padding was going to be around $1,000, was it not?"

"I don't know. I didn't discuss it with them. Bob did."

"This was an arrangement you had made for Bob to get together with people you knew would supply the padding?"

"Yes, I did."

"That was all occurring within a few days prior to the murder of Farah Fratta?"

"Yes."

Prosecutor Siegler on cross-examination asked Thomas, "We've talked about this, you and I?"

"Uh-huh."

"Do you remember telling me, first of all, that this carpet situation came up because Bob Fratta's toilet overflowed about six months prior to his wife's death?"

"I don't remember when it overflowed, but it was either the commode or the bathtub."

"But it was about six months before Farah Fratta was killed?"

"It could have been, yeah."

"You're not the person who made any kind of agreement with Bob Fratta as to how much it might cost if somebody was going to put in a carpet or padding, are you?"

"No."

"As a matter of fact, after Bob Fratta got arrested and that $1,000 was found in the glove compartment of his car, you had a conversation with Bob Fratta about that $1,000, didn't you, Mr. Thomas?"

"Seemed like we did."

"Do you remember Bob Fratta telling you that the $1,000 was to pay you for the carpet?"

"No, he was going to pay for it, the padding."

"That's what he told you?"

"Yeah."

"Because he had already bought the carpet with his Discovery Card from Sears?"

"Yeah, I think he bought carpet from Sears."

"So he told you the $1,000 cash that was in his car that night of his wife's murder was to pay for padding to put in his house?"

"Yes."

The defense called Detective William Valerio to the stand.

"I want to direct your attention to that time when you were doing your interview with Robert Fratta and it was being videotaped," Defense Attorney Ackerman said. "Do you know what I'm talking about?"

"Yes, sir."

"During that particular interview you inquired of Mr. Fratta about life insurance policies on the life of Farah Fratta that might have been payable to him?"

"That's correct."

"And he told you, did he not, that there were none."

"Yes, that's what he told me."

On cross-examination, Prosecutor Siegler asked, "Now, sir, you know that as a result of what he told you that day that three days later he would then call an insurance company demanding payment? Would that be indicative, perhaps, Detective Valerio, that he wasn't telling you the truth?"

"Yes, it would be."

Another defense witness, George Allison, an accountant who said he was a friend of Bob Fratta's, testified that he was aware that Fratta's wife had brought up sexual deviancies in a psychiatric interview and that Fratta "seemed to be humiliated and hurt" by the knowledge that this had happened.

The defense then rested its case.

TWENTY-NINE

Dr. Lawrence Abrams, a clinical psychologist in private practice, was the final witness of the guilt-innocent phase of the Bob Fratta murder trial. The state called Abrams as its only witness in rebuttal testimony.

Abrams said he had evaluated the Fratta family—wife, husband and children—at the request of the family court judge who would preside over the divorce-custody trial scheduled for November 28, 1994. The death of Farah Fratta on November 9, 1994, slightly over two weeks before the trial was to begin, had removed that case from the family court docket and ended Dr. Abrams's psychological evaluation of the Fratta family before it was finished.

He was in the process of evaluating Amber Fratta at the time, having consulted with all other family members.

Dr. Abrams had first seen Farah Fratta in February 1994 and last saw her in April 1994. The father, Robert Alan Fratta, was seen in April and May of 1994.

After completing his personal interviews, Abrams would have made a report to the court judge recommending whether the mother or father should be given custody of the children.

Coprosecutor Casey O'Brien questioned Abrams about his testing of Bob Fratta.

The doctor replied, "I'm frankly going to go over it fairly quickly, and I don't want to get into—I want to be general in what I'm trying to say."

O'Brien asked, "Okay, now in regards to your testing and to your interview, did the subject of deviant sex come up?"

"Depending on your definition of deviant sex, I would say yes."

"Did it also come up during the course of your scoring of those tests that you gave?" the prosecutor asked.

"Not directly. There's certainly something given the allegation."

"What is sexual masochism?"

"It's generally considered the use of sex in some negative form or some pain or discomfort to the individual," said Abrams. "Generally, it's considered to have two components: One form of sexual masochism is related to people that love to be near the edge of death to get excited sexually. And then there's a general grouping of humiliation, suffering, beatings, whippings, some class of degradation or some suffering of an individual. This seems to be required to cause sexual excitement, so both of those fall under sexual masochism."

O'Brien asked, "Did you make any particular findings as a result of your conversations, particularly with Mr. Fratta, and in regards to sexual masochism?"

"Yes, sir."

"Tell us what they were. I don't want you to go into specific acts."

"Well, he had some desire at some point in his life to be involved in both types," the psychologist said.

"And did he indicate to you, in fact, that he engaged in them?"

"Yes, sir."

"With whom?"

"His wife."

"What's coprophilia?"

Abrams explained, "Coprophilia has to do with interest in body excretions, essentially. Philia meaning 'interest in,' copro meaning 'the body' itself and excrements from feces to menses, even nose, mucus, and other things."

"What's paraphilia?"

"That's generally a term referring to any of the philias. There are a number of different areas of interest, which the word philia refers to. Para is a general term for any of those. It groups them together."

"And they are all associated with sexual activity?"

"Yes, sir."

"Of gratification in some respect."

"Yes, sir."

"During the conversation with the defendant, did you have anything, findings, based upon what he told you and how you evaluated that in regards to this coprophilia or paraphilia?"

"Yes, sir."

"Tell us generally again—I don't want to go into specific acts—tell us what it was you found."

Dr. Abrams replied that his impression was that Fratta did participate in coprophilia and other philias, including coprophagy.

"What is that?"

"That's eating of some of the body excretions."

"I'm sorry I asked that last question. I want to ask you specifically some questions in regard to his position on the marriage and women."

"All right."

"Can you tell us, during the course of your discussion with him, did he give you any indication about what kind of marriage he wanted?"

"Well, at the time I talked to him, the only marriage he saw that might work for him was an open marriage."

"What was he telling you that an open marriage was?"

"Open marriage meant essentially both partners could have sexual affairs as they wanted to without any sense of jealousy, supposedly occurring in an effective marriage. He wanted to be able to see his children, so he felt like that was one way to stay with the kids and not have to get divorced and still get away from his wife."

"But he would get to see other women and have affairs with other women?" O'Brien asked.

"Yes, sir."

"But stay with his wife."

"Yes, sir. Even in separate parts of the house."

O'Brien paused to jot down a note. "All right. What was his attitude towards his children and sex?"

"Well, there was one incident, one discussion point, that was very unusual."

At this point, Defense Attorney Charlton's objection to any discussion that had no relevance to the issues was sustained by the judge.

"Let me talk about his representations to you in

his feelings towards women. All right?" O'Brien continued.

"Yes, sir."

"Can you tell us did you develop any impressions as a result of your conversations or tests concerning his attitude towards women?"

"Yes, sir. I did."

"What were they?"

The psychologist said that women were seen by Fratta as "somewhat little girls, somewhat passive.

"He saw them as somewhat constricted. He had some need to dominate what he saw as his 'little girl.' "

O'Brien asked the doctor, "When you are talking about his little girl, are you talking about his child or his wife?"

"He was seeing women that way."

"As children?"

"As little girls," Abrams explained. "Children, childlike perhaps. Dominant. Not necessarily passive, but agreeable to what he wanted. He had some desire to use female bodies to his own desire."

"You mean as his plaything?"

"That would suffice, yes, sir," said Abrams, "I'm trying to avoid specifics."

"How was he in regards to being responsive, in regards to being open and honest and things like that?"

"He was an evasive individual. Sneaky would fit him. And he was particularly sneaky about his feelings. He didn't want them to show. He didn't want his attitudes about sexuality to show. He was generally evasive, concerned with protecting himself, putting up a shell."

O'Brien shifted to another manner of conduct. "All right. What's a narcissist?"

"Narcissism in its purest form is someone so in love with himself or herself that everything in the world around them would just revolve around that person. That person's needs would be the most important thing. Any disruption of those needs would result in anger from the narcissus, sometimes violent anger."

O'Brien asked, "What were your impressions in regard to that word as it fits Bob Fratta?"

Glancing at his notes, Dr. Abrams replied, "The tests suggested somewhat I would call primitive narcissism. Mr. Fratta, he was mostly concerned with himself. He wouldn't fit the full-fledged diagnosis of narcissistic personality, but he had a lot of traits of being concerned with himself first. Other people's needs coming in second, not even being recognized very well. In other words, I need this from you and I need that from you and he just wouldn't hear it, he just wouldn't hear it. It's impossible if it crossed his needs. I have this down in my notes."

When he asked his next question, O'Brien knew he was getting onto a subject that would require caution from him and the psychologist to keep away from the "specifics" that neither he nor the doctor wanted to explore.

"Man and woman, food connected. What do you mean by that?"

"He didn't see man and woman as communicating very well. That was both from testing and interview, but he did on the testing show some perception, there was a food connection between men and women. And I think, well, on some issues on the matter you don't want to go into. Usually I report on each individual."

"Did you do that in this case—report each individual in the summary?"

"No, sir.

"What happened?"

"Before I finished examining the little girl, the mother was killed and the custody case came to an end."

"So your work was moot at that point?"

"That's correct."

O'Brien leaned back in his chair and asked, "You have occasion at some point during the course of your work to confer with the lawyers of both sides, don't you?"

"Yes, sir. I solicit information from both lawyers usually."

"Okay, is it also a practice of yours to alert the lawyers even before you write the report something about in regards to what your recommendation to the court might be?"

"Sometimes, if I think there's a chance for the case to settle out of court without my having to write in the case five reports, which would be a lot of money. If we can save money, we can save the trial of a custody case. A trial which means the parents hate each other even more and the kids become the spoils that go to the victor. If I can avoid that with general comments to the attorneys about what I think is going to happen in this case, I let them both know.

"It dragged out so long, but I was leaning to what I thought might happen," said Abrams.

"Do you have any idea what the time frame was in regards to your conversations with the two lawyers in relaying to them what your findings would be?"

"No, sir. I do not."

O'Brien pushed ahead. "You do know that it was

interrupted? You never got to actually write the report?"

"That's correct."

O'Brien was ready for the key question, as far as he was concerned. With the doctor's answer, the prosecutor hoped to show to the jury the most likely motive that prompted Bob Fratta to murder his wife.

"Would you tell the ladies and gentlemen of the jury, Dr. Abrams, what you were going to recommend to the court as the result of the work you did with the Fratta family in regard to the custody of those children?"

The psychologist paused a few seconds. Then he said, "Barring something completely surprising in the tests analysis, which wasn't completed, I would have to recommend the mother without any question."

"And that's what you, in fact, indicated to both of the lawyers?"

"That's right."

Bob Fratta had known before the custody trial even got underway that he had lost, his wife would have the children and he would have child-support payments for a long time. As prosecutors believed, Fratta had her killed nineteen days before the custody trial was to begin.

Defense Attorney Ackerman, beginning his cross-examination of the expert witness, said, "Psychological tests do not give us absolute results, do they?"

"No."

"They have to be interpreted?"

"Absolutely."

The capable defense lawyer appeared to be striving for an answer that would offset the high scores Fratta had made on the MMPI test on the deviant psychology and paranoia scales.

He asked, "Scoring especially on diagnostic devices such as an MMPI have to be considered in the light of which they are given. The interpretation takes that into account?"

"Yes, sir."

"Okay, for example, answers to certain questions might seem inappropriate in the context of someone like me visiting you in your office? May seem appropriate in another context, and therefore a conclusion or suggestion by a certain score on an MMPI might have to be discounted in the evaluator's mind because of certain conditions under which the tests were taken?"

"The doctor could do that if he wanted to," Abrams replied.

Still pressing, the defense lawyer asked, "But there's nothing unethical, nothing wrong with it as long as he makes it clear what he was doing?"

"Exactly."

"So no doctor, no responsible physician or a psychologist could rely solely on that one test to make a determination about an individual's mental state?"

"Should not."

The state closed after Abrams's testimony. The defense said it had no rebuttal testimony to offer.

The lawyers were ready to make their closing arguments and submit the case to the jury for deliberation. The time was getting near when Bob Fratta would know his fate—whether he walked, or went on to face the big question if found guilty: life in prison or death.

THIRTY

Mary Gipp's incriminating testimony all hinged on the "accomplice" law. The judge's charge to the jury explained the legal meaning of "accomplice" and how it must be applied by the jurors. It fell to Assistant District Attorney Casey O'Brien to explain the accomplice issue to the jury panel.

On the morning of April 17, 1996, O'Brien walked over to the jury box and started his closing argument.

"I want to accomplish a couple of things with a brief argument," he began. "First of all, I want to try and clarify what this long legal document is all about [the charge]. There are a couple of things we didn't talk to you about when we selected the jury.

"One of the things we didn't talk about is the term 'accomplice.' Now the reason it is there is because Mary Gipp testified from this chair. The judge has asked you in his court's charge to decide whether or not Mary Gipp is an accomplice to this crime."

O'Brien explained, "One is, in fact, guilty of the crime if they do something [actually] in furtherance of that crime, if they act as a party in the commission of that crime. Did she do that? She said she didn't.

"She said she did not know that Joe Prystash was going to take the telephone. I'm not sure I believe her. I don't know whether or not Mary knew in advance that he was going to need the cell phone and she gave it to him. If, in fact, she gave him the phone knowing what he was going to use it for on that day, then Mary Gipp is an accomplice and her testimony must be considered what is called accomplice testimony because she supplied and implemented that crime, a telephone. If you believe that Mary Gipp did that, then Mary Gipp is an accomplice.

"The fact that Mary Gipp hid the bullets indicates that she is guilty of a crime. The crime is tampering with physical evidence. Did she in fact tamper with bullets? Yes. Did she in fact lose the bullets? Yes. Did she in fact do that intentionally? Yes. And with that we have no bullets."

Gipp already had been given immunity from a charge of tampering with evidence in exchange for her testimony to the grand jury and at the trial and therefore could not be prosecuted.

"In that regard, I don't have a whole great deal of respect for Mary Gipp. Mary Gipp could have stopped this crime, but she didn't do it. I didn't coddle her and she cried. I didn't stop. I didn't give her a chance to compose herself because I don't like her."

O'Brien told the jurors if they found that, in fact, Gipp was an accomplice, it simply meant that they had to find there was additional evidence that corroborated her testimony.

"And that's what that [accomplice under the law] means. That's the decision you make.

"First of all you must decide if she is an accomplice, and if indeed she is an accomplice, what else is there that you heard in addition to her suggestion that Bob Fratta committed this crime?

"We had all sorts of testimony from other sources. She was one of many. She was one of forty-five people who testified in this case. Now, the bottom line in this convoluted document is did the defendant Robert Fratta hire either Joseph Prystash or Howard Guidry to kill his wife on November 9, 1994?

"That's what that convoluted document asks you to decide. Is he guilty, and have we found sufficient evidence to prove to you beyond a reasonable doubt that he is?

"That's all that thing says." O'Brien indicated the charge-to-the-jury document.

In addition to Gipp's testimony, O'Brien said, there were witnesses who testified to seeing Prystash and Bob Fratta at the President and First Lady gym about two o'clock on that Wednesday afternoon, November 9, 1994.

"Who's with Prystash at two o'clock in the afternoon? What's discussed at two o'clock in the afternoon?"

Then he took the jury step by step over the movements and actions of Prystash and Guidry on the murder afternoon and evening, from the time they left their apartments until they returned after the killing.

O'Brien continued, "Interesting questions: How do they know where Farah Fratta lives? How do they know what time Farah is going to get home? How do they know what her daily regimen is? Who told them there was a playhouse in the backyard for hiding? Who gave them the layout of the garage? Who gave them all the information necessary for that plan?

"You heard crime-scene detectives say the house wasn't broken into, her purse wasn't disturbed, she wasn't raped. Howard Guidry is a thief. He's a bank robber. This wasn't for her money. This was for her death. This was an assassination these men were working. . . .

"Corroboration? Corroboration? You bet your life!"

Defense Attorney Michael Charlton argued that the state did not present its evidence fairly.

"It is not fair what you are being asked to do, and I will base my arguments solely on the evidence that came to you because it is absolutely not fair what is going on in this courtroom.

"You have been presented with pieces, not complete pictures. Pieces taken in isolation, pulled out of context to show a guilty picture. But when you put them in context, there are other explanations that are equally as viable, that do not show that Robert Alan Fratta is guilty of the offense of capital murder.

"Go to the pistol that Mr. O'Brien was using so much. Sure, if you found somebody with a pistol that belonged to the defendant in the commission of a murder it would look suspicious. Actually, we find out that the pistol was in the hands of those people six months before the offense occurred. And when Robert Alan Fratta wanted it back, they wouldn't give it back to him. Mary Gipp says that gun was given to Joseph Prystash for work on Mr. Fratta's car.

"The money situation. Yes, $1,000 in a glove compartment in a car would look suspicious until you found out there were other purposes for which the money was to be spent. Mr. Fratta needed to put carpet in his house.

"If you go on to the phone calls, the state's theory

in the case revolving around the phone calls, the fact that he was responding to so many phone calls, even his own son Bradley testified his daddy was always returning phone calls, always getting pages, always going to the telephone."

Concerning Fratta's alleged sexual deviancies, Charlton said Farah Fratta did not mention them to her physician when she was being treated for depression, did not mention them until later when involved in the divorce.

"The complete picture starts to tear down the state's motive, the state's theory, the state's whole idea of how the case came about. . . . The biggest gap of all has to be Prystash and Howard Guidry. Cross-examination is the engine of truth. It is how lies are uncovered. It is how the truth is brought to citizens like yourselves.

"Cross-examination is the fundamental element of what makes criminal trials fair and you haven't seen it. You are being asked to take on faith what Joseph Prystash and Howard Guidry told the police. You have no real idea whether they, in fact, said it. You have no idea that considerations may have been offered. You have no idea whether there are confessions that were coerced, and you have no idea anything at all about the circumstances under which those statements are made. Because you never heard from those individuals.

"You have no way of knowing that because you didn't see them on the witness stand. It is that that angers me so much. You have no way to understand whether any of these people providing evidence in the state's case are telling you the truth.

"You are being asked to render a verdict without the fundamental tool with which we have to determine the truth in a courtroom, the right to confront and to cross-examine both people who would testify against you. The right to expose the liars they are. Without that, you are being asked to take everything on faith. You are being asked to put a man's life in balance without determining whether those people have told the truth."

Kelly Siegler said that the defense was begging for mercy. "Everything you just heard Mr. Charlton say is that they are begging you for mercy, and I want you when you go back there to show just as much mercy to this man who sits here before you today, as much mercy as he showed to his wife when he had her killed. Bob Fratta pulled the trigger that exploded the brain of his wife just as surely as he is sitting here today.

"Maybe he didn't actually pull the trigger. He used tools or pawns to do it. But it's the same thing.

"We told you when we began this whole process that this would be a circumstantial evidence case. And now you know after forty-five witnesses and five days of testimony, that a circumstantial evidence case can be stronger and better and more convincing and more convictive than any other case in the world. It ain't going to get any better than what you have in this case.

"Every single piece of evidence points in one direction, and it all points solely and simply to that man who sits before you today.

"Mr. Charlton would have you to believe that the only evidence the state could ever have would be to put on that witness chair Howard Guidry and Joe Prystash. Sure would love to do that. There is just one small problem with doing that. In order for us to put in that chair Howard Guidry or Joe Prystash, you wouldn't have been able to stomach the deal we would have to cut.

"Everything that Howard Guidry and Joe Prystash did in this offense, Bob Fratta is guilty for, too.

"One of you asked this question, 'Why would a man like Bob Fratta do this?'

"You probably all wonder that. I mean, look at him. He's nice looking, he's well built, he looks successful. He was a police officer. He made a good living. He had a good marriage. He had a wife that loved him once. He had three healthy, beautiful, intelligent children. He had a mother who loved him, and a sister who loved him. He had it all. He had a lot more than some of you have, but to that man it wasn't enough.

"You can't understand that and will never understand that. Don't even try to figure him out. There's no way you could ever figure him out. There are some people born that none of us will ever understand. You don't know what makes him tick.

"All you know is that he's missing something that all of you have. He's missing a conscience. Start with that when you try to figure out all about Bob Fratta.

"When I made the opening statement last week, I told you what the motive of this man would be in having his wife killed.

"First of all, simply out of hatred. He told his doctor, 'In the beginning she was sweet and innocent. I loved her back then because she did everything I wanted her to do.' Then when she quit doing everything he wanted her to do, he began to hate her.

"He thought he owned her. He bought and paid for her. No one else is going to reap the benefits of what he paid for.

"That was the first motive.

"Then the divorce came, and in the divorce came the deposition, and in February 1993 for the very first time Farah Fratta admitted publicly the disgusting, revolting sexual acts that this defendant required as part of her service as a wife. This is not just a divorce case. That ain't what this is all about. This is about a man who couldn't stand to lose because a wife decided to leave him and make her own life.

"He didn't want those kids in the beginning. He didn't even want custody. The only reason he decided to sue for custody in the end is because he didn't want to pay child support. Paying child support would have put a dent in his partying pocket. He's not a normal father or husband who got outraged by what happens in a normal divorce.

"Farah Fratta never told a soul about all of those things until his lawyer asked her about it in the divorce case.

"Before that she never told anybody. They wanted you to think she made it all up in the heat of the divorce just to make him look bad. You know it's not so.

"Other motives: money, too, a $100,000 life insurance policy, when Farah was dead; a $135,000 overseas trust account to the benefit of the kids that he and his wife were named on.

"That's $235,000. To a man whose wife's life is only worth a Jeep and a $1,000, a quarter of a million is a fortune. You have to believe based on what you understand about this defendant that greed was also a motive. Finally, he wasn't going to let her beat him.

"Do you think it was just a coincidence they were going back to court November 28 and Larry Abrams told you that he let the lawyers know who he was going to say should get the custody and that was Farah? Do you think it was just a coincidence that nineteen days before that day in court is the day that he makes sure she is executed?"

Siegler then pointed out that the insurance claims clerk had testified that when Fratta called her three days after the murder to say, "Where's my money?" he had no idea the beneficiary on the policy had been changed from him to the three children.

At 2:28 P.M. by the clock on the courtroom wall, Judge Burdette announced that the jury had indicated it had reached a verdict. Deliberations had lasted for not quite an hour.

The jury was returned to the courtroom and the jury foreman handed the verdict form to a bailiff, who gave it to the judge.

The judge, after instructing Fratta to stand, read the verdict:

"In case No. 712409, the case styled the State of Texas versus Robert Alan Fratta, the verdict of the jury is as follows: We, the jury, find the defendant Robert Alan Fratta guilty of capital murder as charged in the indictment."

The judge announced that the punishment phase of the case would begin the next morning before the same jury.

* * *

That night at home, little Bradley Fratta said to his grandfather, Lex Baquer: "I don't care if my daddy stays in jail forever. Daddy lied to me. He paid the bad guys to kill Mommy."

THIRTY-ONE

The day after Robert Fratta was found guilty of capital murder, the punishment phase of the trial to determine whether he would be sentenced to life in prison or death by lethal injection moved along rapidly.

The state's opening witness was a television reporter named Dan Lauck, who testified that Fratta had shown no remorse during a lengthy interview with several TV and other media reporters. The interview took place on the parking lot of the sheriff's department homicide office when Fratta emerged from a long session of questioning by detectives that had started the previous night after his wife's murder.

Lauck said, "He was willing to talk, which the reporters considered unusual. Most people who are a suspect in a murder case don't want to talk to reporters. Normally they try to leave as soon as possible. He seemed in no hurry to leave."

The newsman estimated that Fratta answered questions for almost thirty minutes. Lauck said he had heard from investigators that the suspect showed no signs of remorse while being questioned.

"I asked him if he showed any remorse during the

questioning session. He said everything was some-what of a blur and that he did not show any remorse to the investigators."

A lengthy and unedited videotape of the press conference was introduced by the state. An objection by the defense was overruled. The jury viewed the tape. It showed a smug, smiling, sometimes even laughing Bob Fratta, seemingly basking in the spot-light.

The state rested after the TV reporter's testimony.

Called as the first defense witness was Steven Lam-bardi, a Missouri City, Texas, firefighter who was a coworker and friend of Fratta. He said he and Fratta first met in New York, where both were from origi-nally.

Lambardi said he had been in the wedding party when the Frattas had married, and was the godfather for one of the children, Daniel.

Defense Attorney Ackerman asked, "You say you are here for the kids. Explain to the jury whatever you mean by that."

The witness said, "These kids, since they have been born, have been going through hell. You know, they were very young when their parents separated and started going through a divorce. It was a bitter custody battle. Shortly thereafter, their mother was tragically murdered. A short period after that, their father was arrested for hiring someone to commit that murder. After that, Bradley comes and testified in court. Now his father has been convicted of hiring someone to kill his wife, their mother."

Lambardi said he thought the jury should consider

the children and a life sentence when deciding on their father's punishment.

John Friedbauer, a building superintendent for a hospital in Poughkeepsie, NewYork, testified he had known "Bobby" for twenty-six years. They attended school together from elementary to high school.

"Bob was a very upstanding person, very trustworthy, reliable. He was a hard worker. His father passed away and he worked a lot of hours."

Under cross-examination, the witness admitted that in the past twenty-one years he had not had much contact with Fratta.

There was also Cynthia Friedbauer, who had known Fratta since he was ten years old; they had dated in their teens.

"Bob was the only boy in the neighborhood my mom was comfortable with me spending any time with."

There was Fred Denvuko, of Westbury, Long Island, who was Fratta's coach in junior high school. "He was a really nice, respectful, a polite athletic-looking kid that you would want to spend time with. He took part in pole vaulting and sprints."

Mark Cunningham of Abilene, Texas, a clinical forensic psychologist in private practice, was hired by the defense to make a psychological evaluation of Fratta.

He said he interviewed Fratta in jail two separate times for over ten hours in all. He had questioned friends, relatives and coworkers and an ex-girlfriend of Fratta in making his evaluation. He also studied the previous evaluations made of Fratta, viewed a portion of a police video, reviewed records of a temporary custody hearing, and read Farah Fratta's deposition.

He testified that based on his evaluation there was very little likelihood that Fratta would constitute a threat of future danger if confined in the state prison.

Michael Edens, who had testified in the guilt-innocence phase of the trial, was asked by the defense lawyer if he thought Fratta would constitute a danger to anyone in the future.

"A thousand times no," he said.

Prosecutor Kelly Siegler on cross-examination of Edens asked, "Do you remember talking to the police, Mr. Edens, on the night you took Mr. Fratta to your house and you all had the conversation about the card you had on your refrigerator? You know which conversation I'm talking about?"

"Yes, ma'am."

"Do you remember telling the police . . . put[ting] it in your statement, and telling me that night Bob Fratta said something to you that made you believe he was a threat to your very life?"

"Sarcastic comment."

"Is that what you told police, that you thought it was just sarcastic?"

"Yes."

"You told the police that you were afraid for your life?"

"I was afraid, yes ma'am."

* * *

A hush fell over the courtroom when Betty Baquer, fifty-nine, mother of the slaying victim, took the witness chair.

Kelly Siegler immediately got to the heart of the matter. She asked, "Could you tell the jury, please, how the death of your daughter has affected the grandchildren?"

"We have our good days, and they have their good days, bad days. Little Amber, who will be six next month, the next morning when we told her, told the kids they no longer had a mother, she puts her little finger up, says, 'Please, Grandma, please. Please take me to see my mommy just one more time.' And I promised her and the two boys that we would take them to see their mother one more time."

"Can you tell me, Mrs. Baquer, how the loss of Farah has affected your son, Zain?"

"Zain is very angry. He lost his best friend because we just had the two children."

"And can you tell us how the death of Farah has affected your husband, Lex?"

"Lex and Farah were very close. He always called her Baby, his 'Baby.' She always will be his baby. He had to take early retirement to help bring up these three children because we are determined to give them all the love, affection, whatever they needed— not that their mother never gave them any, but they never got any from their father."

"How old is your husband?"

"Sixty-two."

"And how has this affected you and your husband in the respect you are now raising these three children?"

"We don't have a life anymore, thanks to that monster right there."

Defense Attorney Charlton objected to the remark and the judge sustained the objection, instructing the jury not to consider the remark.

"How are you handling this, Mrs. Baquer? How is it affecting you?" Siegler continued.

"I have a hard time. I think of my daughter daily. But Amber helps me a great deal. I see a lot of Farah in Amber, her ways."

Defense Attorney Ackerman cross-examined the mother.

"Good morning, Mrs. Baquer."

"Good morning."

"The children are doing very well in school, are they not?"

"Yes, they are.

"Do they ever get to see their Grandmother Gloria and Aunt Jill?"

"No."

"Do you prohibit that?"

"Yes, I do."

"That's all."

On re-direct, Siegler asked, "Mrs. Baquer, did Bob Fratta's mother ever come to Texas to see these children before all this happened?"

"She never came down for the wedding."

"Has never come to Texas [to see the children]?"

"No, the answer is no."

Ackerman asked on re-cross-examination, "But you know, don't you, that the children visited her in New York on several occasions?"

"That was because they were taken by the father."

"Farah went along on those trips?"

"I believe Farah went, yes."

* * *

Both the state and the defense closed. Arguments on punishment would begin on April 22, 1994.

THIRTY-TWO

The tension was high in the courtroom as Defense Attorney John Ackerman rose to make the first argument which, at best, might save Bob Fratta from the death sentence. The best he could get was life in prison.

Fratta's mother and sister were present, as were Lex and Betty Baquer.

Ackerman began by telling the jurors he was nervous and afraid—"afraid that I won't be able to make the arguments to you that I need to make to you on behalf of Bob Fratta. I'm afraid that I won't find the right words. I've made choices about the things that I want to speak to you about, and I hope I've made the right choices. My fear is that maybe I haven't.

"The responsibility that weighs on my shoulders and my head this morning is one that I would like to have over with. The Baquer family sitting right there has lost a daughter who they loved deeply. I understand the deep grief they are feeling, I do. There are times that grief must be nearly unbearable for them, to have to sit in the courtroom and watch as the death of that beloved daughter is played out before you in court must be a tragic and horrible experience to go through. My heart goes out to that family. . . .

"I also feel and understand the grief and the pain of the Fratta family, who also have had to sit in this courtroom and listen to the things that were said about a son and a brother.

"She has in effect lost a son. At the very best, her son, her only son, will be a prisoner for the rest of his life.

"I also understand the pain and I understand the shame of my client, Bob Fratta. He grew up in a good family. He was given good values.

"He was not able to accept what he felt was the loss of his children. Then came the day of the deposition that you've heard about. Farah Fratta in that deposition said some vile and horrible things about Bob Fratta. Whether those things were true or not, they made him upset. They made him angry. They hurt him. They humiliated him. Bob Fratta couldn't bear this. He became a different person. He became obsessed with his divorce and his custody issues.

"Not only did he become obsessed, he became reckless. Started asking people to help him to solve what he saw as an unsolvable problem and by doing that he had to know that those conversations would become common knowledge.

"He was going around asking people to help kill his wife or to find someone who would do that for him. He had to know if Farah Fratta was killed, the finger of suspicion would inevitably and ultimately point in his direction. He was a reckless and a desperate man who was not himself. . . .

"What happened here was a once-in-a-lifetime convergence of circumstances that created an explosion that will never happen again in his life. He will never havc a wife and three children again. He will never have a marriage that begins to fall apart again. He will never be put back into that corner that he felt himself in 1994. It will never happen again, nor the violence that resulted from it.

"Prosecutors won't be able to point at one time in Bob Fratta's life other than this case where he committed a criminal act of violence, not one. The rest of Bob Fratta's life will be spent in prison.

"There simply is no reasonable basis upon which you can conclude that he will constitute a continuing threat to society. If he had been a violent person, during those several months in the Harris County jail you know we would have heard it.

"What you will probably hear a lot about when the prosecutors talk to you is Bob Fratta's sexual behavior. Even if you believe it is true, it is not violent behavior.

"It is not even criminal behavior. It is simply revolting and disgusting, but it's not violence and it's not criminal.

"Is there an excuse for what happened here? No. Is there an explanation? I think so. I think what I told you about the once-in-a-lifetime convergence of circumstances is an explanation, but just an explanation and not an excuse.

"It's an explanation for all of us to understand, because we need to understand what happened and how it happened."

One of Casey O'Brien's knees had been jerking up and down as Ackerman made his plea to the jury. The prosecutor then rose and walked to the jury box. "I'm about as angry as I've been in my whole life," he began. "You probably watched my knee going up and up. I can't wait to stand up here and tell you what I think. I can't wait to tell that it's time for him to accept the responsibility.

"You are not the ones that are guilty, although we have heard this guilt trip laid on you for the last forty-five minutes.

"Shame. That's what Mr. Ackerman told you Fratta feels. Shame. I don't think so. I don't think he has a conscience. I think you have to have a conscience to feel shame and to feel remorse. He doesn't have one.

"I want to talk to you about that third issue. The issue of whether there is sufficient mitigating circumstances that would warrant life other than death. What do we know about his character? Who was he in November of 1994? A policeman and fireman."

O'Brien read the oath that Fratta had taken: " 'To serve mankind, to safeguard lives and property, to protect the innocent . . . and the peaceful against violence and disorder.'

" 'I will keep my private life unsullied as an example to all, develop self-restraint and be constantly mindful of the welfare of others. . . .'

"You know in 1985, when he became a public safety officer, he took an oath. Is there a paragraph that he didn't violate? What he did in November 1994 was the height of cowardice. I wish that man had the conscience that Mr. Ackerman said he does."

Kelly Siegler gave the final argument for the state.

"When we talked to you so many weeks ago about how you felt about capital punishment and the death penalty, each and every one of you told us that if the crime required it and the defendant required it, you would vote in such a way that the death penalty would be assessed.

"Some of your words are going to come back to haunt you today because some of the things you told us are very familiar when you think about the facts of this case.

"You told us that people who don't deserve the death penalty are people who have decency and honor and compassion in their hearts. This defendant has none of those.

"You told us the lack of remorse is the one thing that you believe more than anything else where the death penalty would be appropriate. This defendant, in spite of all his good lawyers, good arguments and all their books and all their questions, they couldn't come up with any remorse. Bob Fratta has no remorse. He has never felt remorse.

"As far as mitigation, there is no mitigation. He had everything in life. His intelligence level—look at it.

"He's more intelligent than most of the people in this courtroom and look how he wields his intelligence.

"Deviously, diabolically, premeditatively planning to use other people to his benefit. Don't you think a defendant like that is someone who would completely take advantage of anybody he's surrounded with for the rest of his life, whether it's in prison or whether it's in the free world with the rest of us?

"This is not the typical capital murder defendant. Not the typical capital murder case. You would probably have expected to hear about a defendant who went into a 7-11 store, held up the clerk at gunpoint, shot the clerk because he needed money, maybe for drugs, something like that. Don't you think this crime is so much worse than that kind of capital murder could ever be?

"This defendant's greed, his consuming greed and consuming hate for his wife, do you think those things have gone away? Do you think Bob Fratta has learned a lesson and that he hates no more? What burns inside Bob Fratta, that hate, that greed, it hasn't changed.

"It's never going to change in spite of his being raised by two wonderful, loving parents and having everything that life has to offer.

"He's grown up to be this way just because he is this way. You can't fix it. You can't change it. You can't understand it.

"You think there's a worse capital murder case than this one? The murder for hire, your very own wife, a woman you've had children with, a woman you've lived with for years and years?

"How can it get any worse? Of the three involved in this case—this defendant, Howard Guidry and Joe Prystash—who do you think if you had to choose, most deserves the death penalty? There can't be any doubt in your mind that who's the most culpable, the most planning, the most devious, the most diabolical. Why did he do it?

"Because Farah was expendable. He didn't need her anymore. She annoyed him. She stood in the way of what Bob Fratta wanted. Do you think life will always be roses now for Bob Fratta? No, he'll make the same choice again. If he can choose to take the life of his own wife and mother of his children, he can choose to do another criminal act of violence based upon all you know about this defendant.

"If he can manipulate people like police officers and his trusted friends, don't you think he is capable of manipulating the people in prison? We are not obligated to prove to you that this defendant will be both a threat to society in prison and society out of prison. We are not obligated to prove to you that the defendant will be a threat every single day for the rest of his life.

"We are only obligated to prove to you that there is a probability he's going to commit another criminal act of violence.

"Don't you think he can wield influence, though he's in prison, with people on the outside he can still manipulate and still call on. He still has hate and you know who I mean when I say he has a lot of hate for certain people.

"The defense comes in and wants you to spare Bob Fratta because of love for his children. He has no love for those children. The best thing you can do is end this for them as soon as you can. When he's executed, don't you think it's over with for those children? And if you give him a life sentence, then they are going to have to live with the fact that one day possibly their daddy might come home. Why should they have to live with that and worry about that and wonder about that?

"You can't afford to be merciful and give him a chance. The best indicator of how someone is going to be in the future is how they have been in the past. Bob Fratta is not going to change. He's only going to get worse.

"Nothing left for you to do but believe he is a threat and answer those questions in such a way that he receives the death penalty.

"It's time for justice."

* * *

The jury returned its verdict on April 23, 1996.

The jury ruled that there was a probability that Fratta would commit criminal acts of violence that would constitute a continuing threat to society.

They found that Fratta himself actually caused the death of Farah Fratta, or if he did not actually cause the death of Farah Fratta, he intended to kill Farah Fratta or anticipated that a human life would be taken.

It was found that there were not sufficient mitigating circumstances to warrant a sentence of life imprisonment rather than a death sentence.

By answering the first two special issues "yes" and the third "no," the jury had mandated a death sentence for the defendant. Their vote had been unanimous on all three special issues.

Judge Burdette ordered Fratta to stand. He read the verdict to him and declared, "It is the sentence of this court that you be delivered by the sheriff of Harris County, Texas, to the director of the institution of the division of the Texas Department of Criminal Justice, where you will remain confined so that a subcutaneous injection of a lethal substance is administered to your body until your death results."

Fratta's mother and sister burst into sobs.

Lex and Betty Baquer also started crying.

"No punishment could justify our grief," Baquer told reporters, with tears in his eyes. "The least he can do now is apologize to the children."

Defense Attorney Charlton commented to reporters that the jury had been worked into a "frenzy" by the prosecutors. He also referred to a contagious "blood lust" in Harris County—speaking of the county's death penalty record—as a factor in the sentence.

The jury had deliberated about eight hours on Monday and Tuesday before reaching its verdict. It had been sequestered in a hotel on Monday night.

The jurors filed out and each stopped and hugged the Baquers.

THIRTY-THREE

The trials of Joseph Prystash, the middle man in the murder plot, and Howard Guidry, the one who pulled the trigger sending two shots into Farah Fratta, were almost an anticlimax to the lengthy murder investigation. The revelations coming from the murder probe had shocked the city of Houston.

Bob Fratta, the mastermind behind the heinous conspiracy to end the life of the pretty young mother, was already on Texas's Death Row, awaiting the outcome of the endless appeal cycle.

Joseph Prystash went on trial in the 230th State District Court on July 1, 1996, following a hearing on June 4 on a motion by the defense to suppress the confession of Prystash. The motion was overruled and the confession was admitted into evidence.

Kelly Siegler and Casey O'Brien were the prosecutors, and Gerald Borque and Robert Murrow the defense attorneys.

The line-up of witnesses was almost the same as those in the Fratta trial.

One prosecution witness pinned down the time when Joe Prystash had gone to the President and First

Lady gym on the night of Wednesday, November 9, 1994, when Farah Fratta was slain.

The state called Mark Steven Burns, who had been on duty that night at the gym.

Burns said that Prystash usually worked out at the gym in the evening for about an hour and a half. Burns said his office was located in the lobby near the front door. He said, "I have what appears to be a mirror to the people from the outside, but actually is a window so I can see what's going on. Oftentimes members come in and blow past the front desk."

Burns said that each member has a membership card with a bar code on the back that is scanned when a member enters. The log on the computer shows the member's name, type of membership, phone number, whether the account is current and the time and date that the member entered.

Burns said that the assistant who usually keeps watch at the front desk was busy when Prystash entered. "I had to come out of my office when he came in the front door and he was going down the hallway without checking in. I asked him if I could scan him in, and I did so.

"He said to me, 'I'm not going to work out. I'm looking for somebody.' I explained to him I needed to check him in anyway."

Siegler showed Burns State Exhibit 72. It was a computer record showing who checked into the gym on the night of November 9, 1994.

"I want to ask you who is the very last person to scan into your club on that night of November 9, 1994?"

"Joseph Prystash."

"And what time did that happen?"

"At 9:55 P.M."

That was when Prystash was looking for Bob Fratta to get the $1,000 for Howard Guidry in payment for the killing of Farah Fratta. Fratta didn't make it that night. He was being questioned at the homicide office by detectives.

Prystash's confession was introduced into evidence and read to the jury.

In final arguments, the defense attorneys argued that evidence in the case, including the confession, was obtained illegally, sometimes without search warrants or without allowing an attorney to be present when Prystash's statement was taken.

The prosecutors told the jury that detectives followed "the letter of the law" in the case and that investigators fully warned Prystash and carefully observed the other legal requirements.

On July 8, 1996, the jury, after deliberating only seventeen minutes, returned its verdict finding Prystash guilty of capital murder.

During the punishment phase, Mary Gipp testified that Prystash had told her that he broke into Farah Fratta's home and terrorized her with a TAZ, or stun gun, several months before her murder. He was acting on the orders of Bob Fratta, according to Gipp.

The state also called other witnesses, some from out of state, who told the jury about various convictions against Prystash, including seven felonies in Florida. They included his arrest in the Miami, Florida, area in 1976 for the burglary of several underwater diving shops. A former patrol car officer testified that he had caught Prystash in a department store in Dade County, Florida, in 1976 and had to fight to subdue him. He recalled Prystash was armed with a jagged blade knife.

Prystash later had been placed on probation for

some of the burglary offenses. An officer from Montgomery County, Texas, told the jury Prystash was arrested there after an assault on his brother-in-law, but the charge of attempted murder was later dismissed.

Two ex-wives of Prystash testified that they had divorced him. They recalled that Prystash had mood swings and had little remorse about anything. Both former spouses said Prystash seldom held a job and his main ambition was to be a bodybuilder champion. One ex-wife said Prystash mentioned that he would like to be "a mercenary," such as advertised in the soldier-of-fortune-type magazines.

A former head of security at a large hotel testified that Prystash, who worked there for security, was arrested for stealing a $500 microwave from the hotel and served thirty days in jail for misdemeanor theft.

Several witnesses testified that Prystash developed an interest in religion while in jail and attended Bible classes regularly. He had a sincere and interested attitude, one volunteer jail chaplain said.

On July 10, 1996, the jury returned a verdict mandating the death sentence for Prystash.

The seven woman, five man jury deliberated only two hours. Prystash showed no emotion when the verdict was read.

Howard Guidry's capital murder trial started on March 19, 1997, in 230th State District Court.

The same witnesses as in the other murder trials testified. Guidry's confession was read to the jury.

The jury returned a verdict of guilty of capital murder on March 21, 1997.

In the punishment phase, tellers from the Klein

State Bank gave graphic accounts of the robbery on March 1, 1995, in which Guidry and two other men participated. The couple who had seen the bandits fleeing from the bank, and followed their car, also testified.

On March 26, 1997, the jury returned a verdict assessing the death penalty for Guidry. All three defendants are on Texas's Death Row. Guidry was one of seven inmates who tried to escape from the Ellis Prison unit on Thanksgiving night 1998. He gave up when guards started shooting at the fleeing felons. One made it outside, and he was later found drowned in a thickly wooded area.

At the comfortable home in Humble, the home Lex Baquer settled in when he and his family moved from London, Lex and Betty Baquer and their three grandchildren, Bradley, Daniel and Amber, are a happy family.

There is laughter in the house again. Sadness sneaks in far less than in the past.

Baquer is regularly busy with the boys, who play in a soccer league. He goes to all their games. Amber is also happy in school activities. The children reflect their years of upbringing with the Baquers. They are cheerful, extremely polite and well-spoken. The terrible events of that November 9, 1994, are mostly fading into the background.

Lex and Betty Baquer generally avoid the area where Farah Fratta's former home is located.

None of the family will ever forget Farah Fratta and the beautiful person she was.

Acknowledgments

I am grateful for the help given to me during my research of this book by Lex Baquer and Betty Baquer, the devoted parents of murder victim Farah Fratta. I am impressed by the undaunted spirit of Lex Baquer, at the time a grief-ridden man who nevertheless offered his help, night or day, to the investigating homicide officers and prosecutors tracking down and finally convicting the killer.

Baquer, a former Britisher who came to this country because he wanted to live in legendary Texas, is a gentleman of highest integrity and family values.

I also admire the remarkable job the Baquers have done in providing a loving home for the three Fratta grandchildren, Bradley, Daniel and Amber. They are three wonderful youngsters—very bright, well-mannered, doing well in school and after-school activities, moving rapidly again into the world of normalcy after the heart-breaking shock of the nightmarish tragedy that befell their mother on November 9, 1994.

The Baquers assumed this parenting role at a time when people their age ordinarily are looking to their retirement years. Time has rolled back for them, and they are raising a second generation of children and doing it well.

Special thanks to David Deitz, whose friendship gave Farah Fratta some comfort and happiness during the last months of her life. Deitz provided me a candid interview about their friendship that ended in heartbreak with her untimely death.

Thanks also to Ms Rita St. Onge, a nurse and close friend of Farah Fratta, who gave me some additional insight into the lovely person that was Farah Fratta.

My thanks go to the homicide detectives and other officers of the Harris County Sheriff's Department who persevered to untangle the maze of leads and evidence in the Fratta case and later put up, after some initial hesitancy, with my unending questions. I've never met a finer bunch of professional cops. Such men as Sgt. Dan Billingsley, Lt. John Denholm, Detectives Jim Hoffman, Ronald Roberts, William Valerio, and Harry Fikaris, who with others worked countless hours to bring it all together.

My thanks to Harris County District Attorney Johnny Holmes and his hard-hitting staff who were determined from the first day to nail the three murder conspirators with the death penalty.

The prosecution team was Assistant District Attorney Kelly Siegler, the lead attorney, and Casey O'Brien, the Division C trial bureau chief, a good-humored Irishman and veteran murder trial lawyer. I am indebted to Siegler and O'Brien for their help to me.

I cannot say enough about the cooperation and competency I found in Harris County District Clerk Charles Bacarisse's office, particularly the criminal posttrial section. Clerk Ms Myrna Lopez and Ms Donna Valis, the supervisor of posttrial, pulled the cumbersome trial transcripts of all three capital murder cases—Fratta, Prystash and Guidry—and daily for more than a week guided me through them. They are credits to public service.

Deep appreciation goes to Houston freelance photographer Joe D. Draught for his top-notch work and willingness to work odd hours after finishing his regular busy day.

My thanks to Ms Sherry Adams, head librarian for the *Houston Chronicle,* who over the years has been a dependable research source for some of Houston's top crime cases.

Thanks, also, to attorney James M. Beeler, of Victoria, Texas, who was helpful in providing information on Farah Fratta's lengthy custody court battle.

My wife and I are grateful, too, for the splendid Thanksgiving week hospitality and transportation provided by Bob and Judy Bybee of Port Lavaca during our stay in the Houston area.

And, as always, I could not function without my wife Nina's encouragement and patience in the role of travel companion, secretary, counselor, researcher and copy-editor.

I appreciate working with my book editor, Ms Karen Haas, attorney Barbara Bennett and editor-in-chief Paul Dinas. It takes a lot of people to put together a book after it has been written and to keep a writer from climbing the wall.

And I love the big town of Houston—sprawling, boisterous, exciting, demanding, but always tops in Texas hospitality and friendliness.

Bill G. Cox
June 15, 1999

MORE MUST-READ TRUE CRIME
FROM PINNACLE